3 + 4
Equals
Success

Skills and Mindsets Needed for

Career Growth and Satisfaction

By Darren K. Ford

ProCulture Publishing

First Edition

ISBN-13: 978-1497470613

ISBN-10: 1497470617

Contact info:

Darren@procultureconsulting.com

www.procultureconsulting.com

Dedication

This book is dedicated to my beautiful bride of 26 years, Pat, who has supported me throughout my career. With every venture and at every turn, you have been there with ideas and encouragement. Thanks for all you do to keep the family running and, most of all, thanks for believing in me.

Contents

Introduction

Efforts and courage are not enough without purpose and direction.

John F. Kennedy

Do you live on purpose?

You may find that a strange question, but it's a critical question. In fact, it may be one of the most important questions you can ask yourself.

It's hard to stay focused on our life. In our highly technical and fast-paced world, the distractions are endless. With all the good technology has brought us, there is a dark side. We can't "get away". We're always plugged into work and into the world, often wasting time looking at Facebook postings of people we don't even know. Let's face it, life is full of distractions and technology amplifies the volume!

Fighting through all the noise allows you to examine your life and get to that very important question. Do you live on purpose? While it requires a "yes" or "no" answer, it really needs a little more explanation. People hear that question and may have different thoughts about its meaning.

For our purposes in this book, we're going to apply that question to work. In fact, we could even change the question a bit to say, "Do you work on purpose?" Other than simply earning money, do you have a reason to work? It's an important question that everyone must answer.

Think about it. We spend half (sometimes more than half!) of our awake adult life at work. With so much time spent in one area, why wouldn't we want to make sure that time is spent, well, on purpose?

Sadly, too many people trudge into work, mindlessly go through their daily work routine, and then go home. Their work isn't fun. There is no satisfaction. They are simply trading hours for dollars. They give the company some hours and the company gives them some dollars.

Day after day after day. . .

What if you enjoyed your work? What if you had a plan for your professional career? What if you received more than just dollars for your efforts? What if you actually received satisfaction and were excited about the work you perform? Wouldn't that make life better? It would certainly make the day go by faster!

Answering those questions is what this book is all about. We'll seek those answers by concentrating on a few life skills and some pointed questions. Specifically, we'll examine three key skills that can be applied to your work situation and life in general, and four questions you need to ask yourself. Don't worry; I'll also give you the correct answers to those questions!

Doing these things on purpose will result in happiness and satisfaction with your job. You will also reap the benefits of that happiness and satisfaction which include more responsibility, promotions, perhaps a new direction for your professional career, and most likely more money.

3 + 4 Equals Success.

The skills and questions we will explore here aren't new or earthshattering. While the book references research, there's no groundbreaking study or findings here to back up the above equation. In fact, the skills being presented and the questions being asked are all pretty basic. But the power those skills and questions offer? Limitless!

There are numerous books written about each topic that we cover here in just a few pages. Each topic can easily stand on its own with pages and pages dedicated to a deep dive into each subject. After reading this book, maybe your curiosity will be peaked and you will want to explore a topic a little more. I would encourage that.

Our purposes here, however, are a little different. This book is not intended to be an in-depth study of these critical topics. In fact, it's just the opposite. This will be an easy read. The book is short, the points are simple, and the aim is merely to get you going in the right direction. In fact, if you have an hour or two, you can probably finish it in just one sitting.

The objective for this short primer is to get you thinking. Well, it's actually more than that. In addition to thinking, I hope this book spurs you to action. Action that will get you working on purpose.

Are you ready? I hope so. Grab a cup of coffee or soda, pull up a chair, and jump in. I'm confident that, when you read the last page, you'll be happy you did!

1

I'm gonna be an astronaut

"That's one small step for [a] man, one giant leap for mankind." [1]

Those are the first words spoken as Neil Armstrong took the first human steps on the moon. I'll never forget that July 20th night in 1969. I was in Dustin, a little town in south central Oklahoma. I had been following the flight of Apollo 11 on TV news since it had launched four days earlier. I was fascinated with everything space—rockets, planets, stars, and, of course, astronauts.

It was almost 10:00 p.m. and past my bedtime—I was 8 years old—but there was no way I could sleep. After all, I was going to be an astronaut someday and I had to see how you walk around on the moon!

So, earlier in the evening, I claimed my spot right in front of the TV, against the advice of my grandmother. "Move back, Darren. Sitting that close is going to ruin your eyesight," Gannie would say. But there was no pushing me back that night. After arranging my pillows and blanket along with a small nighttime snack, I settled in front of the TV with about an hour to spare.

Then it finally happened—the fuzzy picture showed Neil Armstrong slowly climbing down the ladder of the lunar module. As soon as he took that first step, he uttered that famous (and controversial) first sentence from the Sea of Tranquility on the moon's surface.

Shortly after those first steps it was off to bed for me. Of course, I protested loudly. "I'll never be able to fall asleep, mom!" But with school the next day, I was done for the night and in spite of the excitement, was asleep in minutes.

I continued following Apollo 11 until its splashdown in the Pacific Ocean on July 24.[2] I could not wait to become an astronaut! Hey, maybe I could be the first man to walk on Saturn! With all those rings, that was one cool planet!

By the time Apollo 12 launched just four months later, I had moved on to my next career choice: starting shortstop for the Chicago Cubs. Someday I was going to be a major league baseball player!

Are you surprised that after just a few months I had already changed careers? Don't be. You see, just two months before Neil Armstrong walked on the moon, I wanted to be a racecar driver after watching Mario Andretti win the Indianapolis 500 on May 30.

Over the course of my childhood, I wanted to be a pilot, drive tanks in the Army, be a firefighter, operate huge construction machines like cranes and dump trucks, and be a super spy!

Now, think back on your childhood dreams. What did you want to be when you grew up? Maybe you had ideas like me of going into space, building buildings, or sleuthing around dangerous countries, bringing back top secrets from our enemies.

Maybe some of your early desires were to be a super hero or a wizard. Once you realized these were not real jobs, perhaps you turned to actual careers. Maybe you wanted to be a doctor (I don't like blood so that was out for me), a veterinarian (I like dogs but, again, blood might be involved), or a teacher. How about a ballerina? A scientist?

A few people pick that childhood dream and make it a reality.

According to a LinkedIn study that surveyed over 8,000 professionals globally, only 8.9% of those surveyed work in their childhood dream job.[3] In other words, only one in ten people actually get to enjoy the job they dreamed of when they were six, seven, or ten years old.

When you count those people working in a field related to their childhood dream job, the numbers are a little better with 21% [4] of the respondents falling into this category. Add it all up and about three in ten respondents to the LinkedIn survey can happily say they followed, or almost followed, their childhood dreams.

What about the other 70%? If they didn't follow their childhood dreams of being doctors, dancers, or drummers, where did they land? Well, just about anywhere. Business people, truck drivers, accountants, plumbers, construction workers, politicians, engineers, auto mechanics, real estate agents, news anchors, coal miners, chefs, delivery men, flight attendants......... The list goes on and on to include thousands of jobs that make the world operate.

One of those "everyday" jobs is a Contact Center Representative (known as a CCR from this point on).

How did I end up here?

Of all the childhood dream jobs, do you think a CCR is anywhere in the top 10? Not according to author and Human Resources expert, Alison Doyle. She lists the Top 10 Childhood dream jobs as:[5]

1. Astronaut
2. Musician
3. Actor
4. Dancer
5. Teacher
6. Firefighter
7. Police Officer
8. Writer
9. Detective
10. Athlete

Okay, not in the Top 10. How about Top 15? Nope! Doyle lists

those next five spots as:
11. Vet
12. Scientist
13. Pilot
14. Lawyer
15. Doctor

Maybe the CCR makes it to the Top 50? Top 100? Based on the blank stares I received after asking five young people, "Would you like to be a Call Center Representative when you grow up?", it's probably safe to say that working in a call center isn't even on the radar screen of children.

However, that doesn't mean those children won't ultimately find themselves working in a call center. In fact, U.S. call centers employ approximately 5 million people.[6] Now that's a lot of jobs! According to most experts, employment in the U.S. contact center industry is growing faster than many other industries.

So, if you are reading this book, it probably means you are working in a contact or call center. If you're working in such an environment, have you ever asked yourself this question?

"How in the world did I get here?"

A question for everyone

"How in the world did I get here?" along with the follow-on questions aren't just for call center agents. Everyone can and should ask these questions. While we talk mostly about call centers in this book, the ideas and concepts can be applied to just about any job. Let's face it; does anyone grow up dreaming about being a warehouse worker? A TV repairperson? An accountant? A business professional? Outside of those few astronauts, fire fighters, and ballerinas, we all leave our childhood dreams and end up in a different career. So regardless of where you are today, make it a point to ask these questions (and read the rest of this book)!

Then, more questions begin flooding your mind:

- Am I happy here?
- Why am I still here?
- Is this all there is for the rest of my life?
- Where do I go from here?
- Does it matter that I am here?
- Can I make a difference while I am here?

All great questions which we'll tackle later on in this book. For now, though, let's explore how you got to a call center.

A gradual path

Of course, there's no blanket answer that covers all paths to a call center. Maybe you needed some part-time work and a call center fit the bill. One of my sons spent his summers during his college years in a call center. If that's you, maybe that part-time gig morphed into a full-time, longer term, job.

For others, in a down economy and with call centers growing as mentioned earlier, maybe this was the only job you could find. Working as a CCR was simply a way to support yourself or your family. And even though the economy is starting to pick up, you still find yourself working in the call center.

For others, maybe your march toward your childhood dream of becoming a ballerina or basketball star was interrupted by some life challenge that changed your path from college or some other training ground to this track as a CCR expert.

Whatever the reason, you're in a call center. Day in, day out. Getting to work on time (hopefully!), grabbing that first cup of coffee, adjusting your headset, and taking that first call of the day. Two breaks, a lunch hour, and 70, 85, maybe 100+ calls later, your shift ends. You go home, eat dinner, sleep, and start it all over again the next day.

Let's again ask the question: How did I get here? From the

answers above or any one of dozens of other paths to your current CCR position, it comes down to being deliberate. On your way to becoming a race car driver, astronaut, teacher, famous musician, scientist, engineer, nurse, or whatever you wanted to do in life, you stopped being deliberate and somehow, somewhere, sometime took a detour.

That detour was most likely gradual. It's doubtful that you woke up one morning and suddenly found yourself making or taking phone calls all day long. It just sort of happened. In his book *Start*, author Jon Acuff puts it this way, ". . . I finally woke up one day in a cubicle and realized I'd coasted through the last ten years of my life."[7]

Is there anything wrong with being a CCR? Absolutely not! In fact, I want good CCRs to answer my banking questions, help with a billing problem, or take my order for that new set of knives I saw advertised on TV. The millions of CCRs putting on a headset each and every day play an important part of keeping our society, and our economy, functioning smoothly.

If, however, you unexpectedly find yourself wearing one of those headsets but still have dreams and aspirations of doing something different, keep in mind those dreams don't just happen. It takes work. Often, it takes lots of work! Like most anything of value, you must put in the sweat and effort to attain that career brass ring.

Is this career thing easy? Of course not. Jon Acuff addresses this as well when he writes about leaving the average, easy life path to a life of awesomeness. "[The awesome path] is dangerous too— but the good kind of dangerous. The kind of dangerous through which all great accomplishments must travel. On it are tall mountains, rocky walls, and even an occasional dragon. You're going to get bloodied, your discipline will be tested, and your dreams will be challenged a thousand times over. But ohhhh, it is awesome."[8]

Carnegie Mellon University professor Randy Pausch understands the same concept when he talks about the challenges of brick walls. In *The Last Lecture*, Pausch said, "The brick walls are there for a reason. The brick walls are not there to keep us out.

The brick walls are there to give us a chance to show how badly we want something. Because the brick walls are there to stop the people who don't want it badly enough. They're there to stop the other people."[9]

Yes, some people will have more opportunity or more contacts, and may even have more resources (particularly money) than others. These "more" items might make it easier for them to reach their life goals than you. But if you work hard enough, if you are deliberate enough, you can find your ultimate career path as well.

I know, I know – this is easier said than done. You're probably thinking, "Just be deliberate and I'll get my ultimate career. Yeah, whatever." But that thinking, that attitude is your choice. And that attitude will never get you where you want to go. More about attitude later...........

For now, let's concentrate on what to do as you sit there, headphones on, monitor displaying customer information, preparing to take that next customer call.

Okay, now what? Just turn the page.

2

I am NOT a Contact Center Representative

Regardless of how you got there, you are now a CCR. The question is: What kind of CCR are you? There are many adjectives and phrases we could choose from to describe the type of worker you are:

- Happy or sad
- Passionate or uncaring
- Thinking critically or just going through the motions
- Working hard or hardly working
- Positive or negative
- Engaged or detached
- Joyful or sour
- Proactive or procrastinating
- Driven or lazy
- Self-starter or quitter
- Supportive or obstructive

The list could go on and on and on and . . .

Bottom line, we all have a pretty good idea of what distinguishes a good worker from a bad one. From the words in the paragraph above, words like passionate, thinking, driven, leader, learner – those are the words we use to describe top performing employees. The opposite of those words such as sad, negative, and quitter are words used to describe less-than-desirable employees.

Many factors go into the type of worker we are. What's going on at home and in our personal life? What kind of boss do we have? What is the business environment? Is my company growing or letting people go? Just like the list of words used to describe an employee type, there are multiple factors that have an impact on the type of worker you are.

But what we've just listed are external factors. Whether the economy or your boss, these external dynamics don't have to have a negative impact on your work. What does impact your work, more than any other factor, is an internal influence. It's something you choose. No one or no thing can choose it for you.

Don't have an attitude

Well, that's not exactly right. You should have an attitude. Just make certain that it isn't a BAD attitude. You see, it's the type of attitude that is key!

Let's start our exploration of attitude by reviewing what others have said about the importance of attitude:

> *You cannot tailor-make the situations in life but you can tailor-make the attitudes to fit those situations.*
>
> **Zig Ziglar**

> *Nothing can stop the man with the right mental attitude from achieving his goal; nothing on earth can help the man with the wrong mental attitude.*
>
> **Thomas Jefferson**

> *Attitude is a little thing that makes a big difference.*
>
> **Winston Churchill**

> *Weakness of attitude becomes weakness of character.*
>
> **Albert Einstein**

Which is more important, attitude or ability? According to a Scottish novelist Walter Scott, success depends on both:

> *For success, attitude is equally as important as ability.*

Don't forget—attitude is not just important, it's vital. It's Key #1 to your success.

Key #2? Your attitude is YOUR choice.

> *The greatest day in your life and mine is when we take total responsibility for our attitudes. That's the day we truly grow up.*
>
> **John C. Maxwell**

> *Our lives are not determined by what happens to us but how we react to what happens, not by what life brings us but the attitude we bring to life.*
>
> **Wade Boggs**

No one can choose your attitude for you. No one can force an attitude upon you. Your attitude, how you approach life and other people is up to you and only you.

That's an important concept to remember and practice as you work in a call center (or any other job). As we reviewed in chapter 1, there is absolutely nothing wrong with being a call center representative. Many people enjoy this career and have experienced great success. Perhaps, though, you have bigger or just different plans. Regardless, you are where you are, and now it's your choice how you approach your position. You can grumble about it or choose to take control of your attitude and your actions.

Might this be easier said than done? Maybe. In fact, you might be saying to yourself, "Well, you just don't know my life. And you don't know this job. After all, it's just an old customer service job. How can I have a positive attitude about that?"

Good point, but I have an answer for you. Actually, three answers. Choosing that positive attitude is much easier when you believe in the work you do. How do you believe in being "just" a contact center representative? Three ways:

1. Be the best
2. Know your business
3. Recognize that your job is to help others

I'm #1

Who won the Super Bowl in January of 2013? If you're a sports fan, you'll recall it was the Baltimore Ravens. Who did they beat? Unless you're a big football fan, you probably don't remember that Baltimore defeated the San Francisco 49ers.

Who set the record for most gold medals in a single Olympics in 2008? You probably know it was Michael Phelps. Do you know any of the other swimmers? Probably not.

We celebrate being #1. We give trophies for first place. We give awards to the best players, the best movies, and the best singers.

Can you be the best call center rep? Maybe. Two of my three boys work at a call center. My middle son works as a CCR to help pay for college. His older brother works at the same call center and was rewarded the first parking space right by the front door when he was named "Employee of the Month". This was a huge benefit since parking was a complete mess. So, at least for one month in one contact center, he was the best.

But how does he rank all year or against CCRs from other contact centers? That really can't be measured. Therefore, a better way to measure your "number one-ness" is to measure against yourself. In other words, are you the best you can be?

Why is it important to do your best? Some would argue that it's simply the right thing to do, especially for those people around you. To a certain extent, their success and maybe even happiness depends on you so if you do anything less than your best, you are limiting their success, their potential. And that's just wrong.

How is this wrong? Well, just turn it around. What if your job results are even partly dependent on someone else's work? If they aren't giving it 100% effort, then they could be holding you back from reaching your goals.

What we're talking about here is the Golden Rule. Very simply put, the Golden Rule teaches us to treat others as we would like to be treated. This philosophy, of course, can be applied to many areas in life. Want respect? Then you must respect others. Want to be appreciated? Then you need to appreciate others. Want to be loved? Then you need to love.

Applying the Golden Rule to your work says that if you want people around you to do their best so you can succeed and reach your goals, then you must do your best in order for those around you to reach their goals.

If you don't do your best, you simply end up cheating yourself. Don't do your best to study for that test? You don't get the highest grade possible. Only give 50%, 75%, or even 90% effort at work? Only earn 50%, 75%, or 90% of the bonus you could have received. "Hey, I got $90 but if I would have worked just a little harder, I could have made $100!" Or if you have a really good bonus plan, 90% effort could be the difference between $900 and $1,000!

Doing your best also sets up future success. Og Mandino, author of the bestselling book *The Greatest Salesman in the World* said, "Always do your best. What you plant now, you will harvest later."[1] Oprah Winfrey made a similar comment, "Doing the best at this moment puts you in the best place for the next moment."[2] This is pretty logical, isn't it? The harder you work now, the better your results. The better results now allow even better results later. And so on, and so on . . .

When put in these terms, doing your best simply looks like common sense, doesn't it?

Doing your best helps you get out of bed every morning. Looking forward to the day's work, being confident and satisfied is easier when you know you're doing everything you can do, giving 100%.

What else contributes to your job satisfaction? It's important to understand your company's business and the part you play.

Success depends on me

Do you know your company's business? The answer is probably

yes. You probably have a pretty good understanding of what your company does overall. Maybe you work in a reservation center for an airline. If that's the case, you understand that you help people go from one place to another by plane. Perhaps you load coal into countless cars as you work for one of the railroads that crisscross the country. If this is the case, you understand your company delivers products across the U.S. by rail and that your specific job allows electric companies to keep generating power through the coal it burns.

You get the idea. You are aware of what you do, day in and day out, and have a good understanding of your company's overall mission.

But do you *really* know what you do? And do you *really* know what your company does or what its goals are?

When I worked at a large financial institution that specialized in providing auto loans to consumers, everyone had a good understanding of our business—we gave out car loans. Pretty simple.

Unfortunately, most people did not understand the overall process of providing those loans. They did not know how the Sales and Credit departments worked and were unaware of the costs associated with people who stopped paying their loans. More importantly, our associates had no idea regarding the company's financial status, either how much money we made the previous year or the current year's financial goals.

Granted, part of the problem was a lack of communication from the company. They failed to provide this information to everyone in the organization. Could part of the problem also lie with the employees? Was anyone curious about the financial goals?

Had the employees servicing the loans been aware of the company's aggressive financial objectives, would they be so fast to waive a fee for a customer? Might the Funding department work a little harder or a little faster, approving that one extra loan before the end of the day?

Some people would argue that one single $15 fee would not help the company reach a goal that is in the hundreds of millions of dollars. But what if you have over 1,000 employees working on those fees? And what if each of those employees were able to secure just one extra $15 fee per day? Now that little $15 fee is adding millions of dollars to the bottom line each year!

Having a clear understanding of the entire business and knowing that your individual work has a direct impact on the company's overall success is the second criteria for believing in your customer contact responsibilities.

Want even more job satisfaction? Then you must understand what your real job is.

People Improvement Specialist

During my time at the auto finance company, I had the privilege of teaching a customer service program to many of the employees. I taught both customer-facing employees and people who work "internally", such as the IT department, accounting, and even my own HR group. To begin that customer service teaching, we listened to a discussion between one of our customers and one of our call center representatives.

Sadly, this customer had run into some hard times and was behind in his car payments. We were calling to help this customer get back on track with their payments. Unfortunately for us, the call center representative didn't truly understand her job.

After a few tense exchanges between the two, the customer said,

"I just made a payment. I told you when I would make my next payment. Why do you keep calling me?"

The CCR's response?

"That's what we do, sir."

Well, at least she called him "sir."

Really, that's what the company does? It just calls people and asks for money?

NO!

That customer service representative didn't understand her true job. What she really did, one customer at a time, was help. She answered questions, helped people understand their financial situation, and made them feel comfortable with their auto loan. At least that's what she was supposed to be doing.

In fact, I would tell all of the CCRs that if I were president of the company, I would change everyone's title to People Improvement Specialist. No more account managers or customer service representatives. Everyone would simply have the title of People Improvement Specialist.

Why? Because that's what they did! They improved peoples' lives by helping them make their payments and keeping them in their cars. With that reliable car, our customers could do what everyone desires to do—go to work, strive for their life goals, take care of family, visit friends, and everything else we do using our car.

No matter what you do, no matter what type of contact center you work in or type of calls you make, don't forget that you do that exact same thing—you improve peoples' lives, one person at a time. Sound crazy? It shouldn't. No matter what type of work you do, your outlook on that work can make that work meaningful.[3]

- Vivian, an immigrant from Vietnam, took great pride and satisfaction in her work as a housekeeper in a boutique hotel. How did she find satisfaction in making beds, cleaning toilets, and vacuuming carpets? First, she enjoyed making emotional connections and friendships with her coworkers and hotel guests. She also took pleasure knowing she was helping an away-from-home guest feel comfortable in these strange surroundings. After all, Vivian could relate to these travelers – she was far from home as well.

- A phlebotomist (that's someone who draws blood samples) was found to be happy one day because she had lots of empty tubes lined up just waiting to be filled with blood samples? How can that make the phlebotomist smile? This professional explained that most illnesses are first detected through simple blood tests. So having lots of empty tubes lined up meant this person would have many chances to help people.

- Workers at a call center that raises funds for student scholarships also found joy and satisfaction in helping people. This call center work is particularly hard due to the large number of calls made and the small number of actual donations. But when the CCRs focused on the students they actually helped, their satisfaction and their performance increased!

Martin Luther King, Jr. understood the value of helping people when he said, "All labor that uplifts humanity has dignity and importance and should be undertaken with painstaking excellence."[4] It's not the work that matters, it's the people! The ability to create worth and meaning from your work, wherever you find yourself, lies within you and your ability to see the value of people.

Another way to look at your job is that it's not about you. You are most likely part of a team which is part of a bigger team which is eventually part of the entire organization. Unless you are willing to do your part and do it to the best of your ability, the entire team and the organization falls short of its ultimate potential.

There is a story—some people debate the details or if it actually happened at all—revolving around America's journey to the moon. Several months after President Kennedy challenged America to put a man on the moon and return home, a U.S. congressman was touring the NASA facility in Houston. The cost of getting to the moon and safely back was astronomical and this congressman wasn't convinced that we needed to spend this type of money.

After visiting the NASA complex for the day, this congressman came upon a janitor at the end of the tour. Broom in hand, the janitor was simply sweeping the floor of a large hanger. The congressman walked up to the janitor and asked, "Excuse me. What are you doing here this late? Seems everyone else has gone home." The janitor's response: "I'm helping to put a man on the moon, sir." Then and there the congressman decided to fund the ambitious and expensive moon project.[5]

Wow! This janitor got it! He was just sweeping the floor but realized that his work was helping get America to the moon. He created his own worthwhile work by choosing to believe in his task! He had the bigger picture, which is exactly what Alexander the Great had in mind when he said, "Remember upon the conduct of each depends the fate of all."[6]

Are you getting the picture? Are you starting to see value in your work, regardless of where you are or how you got there?

Unfortunately, some people reading this book are thinking, "Yeah, this all sounds good but really, you don't know where I work. You don't understand my situation. My work just doesn't matter." Is this you?

You may work in a call center where customers are calling you, perhaps ordering the latest "For just $9.95 we'll send you TWO battery operated bug catchers." Now you may not think too much of your call center position but to that person trying to enjoy their backyard without mosquitos, you are doing an important job. In fact, you could say you're improving someone's life by taking that order. At the very least, you're putting a smile on someone's face, bringing them a little happiness.

Maybe your call center is one making outbound calls, trying to collect money on an overdue account. Sometimes this work is not fun, especially when you get an angry customer on the phone. Think, however, how you are helping those people keep their accounts as current as possible, helping them minimize the damage to their credit, which has long-term benefits for their finances and way of life.

No matter what type of customer service representative you are, keep in mind that you are helping people in some manner. You are also helping your company, your teammates around you, and ultimately, yourself.

In the end, you're right: I don't know your situation. Not exactly. But I do know that how you view your job is important and is simply a matter of choice. Your choice! Only YOU can decide the attitude you bring every day. YOU decide how much you know about your company and its goals. YOU decide what type of experience you will provide to your customers each day. Ultimately, only YOU can choose to be a People Improvement Specialist—or not.

It's Not Just Call Centers

While most of this book revolves around those men and women sitting in a cubicle, wearing a headset, and taking/making dozens or even hundreds of calls a day, this idea of making worthwhile work and doing your best can be applied to any job.

How about account receivables and payables? Not only does your company depend on the correct money coming in and going out, your customers and suppliers also need help in keeping their records straight. Making sure all the numbers make sense at the end of a month or year can get tedious, but never lose sight of just how important these functions are.

Do you work in the payroll department? This mindset includes you as well. Not much to add here except, who doesn't want to get paid the correct amount of money, on time?

People working in administration positions, facilities, IT, legal, warehousing, construction, and any job you can name, all of these positions are ultimately responsible for helping people. Each of these positions performs a function that is addressing a need of an individual, a group of people, or the entire company.

The ideas, concepts, and lists presented in this book also apply to people working in the food and retail industries as hosts, counter help at fast food restaurants, stock clerks, and all the other functions that make our society work. Whether selling shirts in a mall or serving shakes at a burger joint, people want a pleasant experience. And you are just the right person to deliver that experience at that point in time!

3

Is this it?

Still reading? Just like choosing to be a People Improvement Specialist, you can choose to keep reading this book . . . . or not. In fact, choice is a theme throughout this short guide. It's your choice how you view life. It's your choice how you approach your job, your boss, and your coworkers. And it's your choice to spend some time investing in yourself by reading this book.

Life is hectic and there are constant demands on our time. But slowing down enough to invest in ourselves is a key to happiness and success. "Investing" will be the primary topic in the second half of this book. For now, I'll simply throw the idea out there. Are you willing to push through all of the noise and distractions to make it to the end this book? While I hope you stick with it to the end, it doesn't have to be my book. There are many great books available to help career choices and professional development. If this one isn't grabbing you, pick up a different one. It's okay; you won't hurt my feelings (well, maybe a little – the point is to do something to help move your career forward). Remember, it's a choice. It's YOUR choice. But I highly encourage you to push onward to the last page in this title.

So, where are we? We've determined that you have landed in a contact center of some sort and it probably wasn't the career path you chose years ago. For whatever reason, you find yourself punching in and out every day and talking to people you'll most likely never meet in person. Now what? Is this it or is there something more? Said differently, maybe you're asking yourself, should I stay or should I go?

To answer the overall stay-or-go question, you probably need to ask yourself a few more questions, such as:

- Can I find a place that challenges me?

- I don't like my job but I like my boss. What if I change jobs and get a horrible manager?

- Can I find more money elsewhere?

- I'm not learning anything here. Can I find a job that helps me grow professional? Personally?

- The environment here is toxic. There are too many negative people here. Is it possible to find a more uplifting corporate culture?

These are just a few questions you need to explore. Keep in mind there are no right or wrong answers to these questions. Each person, each job, each manager, and each environment – they are all different and are perceived differently for everyone reading this book. After all: "One man's ceiling is another man's floor."

The one question that does have a right answer is this:

Am I just trading hours for dollars here?

If you are not totally engaged in your current job, you may simply be going through the motions of your daily activities. You are giving your company a few hours of your time and they are giving you a few dollars. You're making a simple (and boring) trade, hours for dollars, and are most likely staring at the clock, anxiously awaiting each break, lunch and quitting time.

If this is you, then there's no way you can flourish where you are. The longer you trade hours for dollars, the harder it becomes to get up in the morning and go to work. You may start showing up late, maybe just a few minutes but late nonetheless. Your breaks might extend by just a few minutes. Then you find yourself taking a day off here and there. Finally, either by your choice or the company's, you end up taking your skills and abilities someplace else.

The entire time you're trading those hours for dollars, you won't be happy, your boss won't be happy and your customers won't be happy. You're cheating the company (and yourself) of a full day's efforts, and spinning into a downward spiral.

You know some of these people. They are the workers who have already quit but just haven't told anyone and have decided to tolerate their job until something better comes along. Don't let this be you!

Back to the question that started this section: Should I stay or should I go?

NO ONE can answer that question but YOU. You are the only person on the planet who knows your exact situation – your own skills, attitudes, desires, bosses, opportunities both inside and outside of your current job, and everything else that goes into making career and life decisions. Yep, this is one time where "It's all about YOU!"

If you believe the last paragraph (and I hope that you do), then let's get through a little exercise. If you don't believe the last paragraph, then I would suggest that you go back and read it again.......... Then come back to this spot to start the exercise.

Are you with me?

Let's get started:
- Pull out a pad of paper and make two columns: one titled Pros with the other titled Cons.
- Think about your current job.
- List as many items on each side of the paper as you can.
- Take a short break and then check your list again, adding anything that you may have forgotten.

Are there more reasons to stay at your current job than there are to leave? Is that okay? After all, it's just a customer service position (or whatever job title you have). Keep in mind that there's nothing wrong with a customer service position or any other job for that matter. In your case, you're not simply a CCR; you're a People Improvement Specialist!

That may be the only reason you need to justify a long-term stay at your call center -- you're helping people, in some way, one person, one call at a time. However, there are other good reasons to stay. For example, unlike many jobs in this world, when you're at work, you work, but when you leave the office, you can actually leave the office behind. No worrying about deadlines, projects, or being "on call" like some jobs. Some jobs require people to always be available, always think, always worry about "the next big thing." With most call center jobs, when you punch out of the

When Is a Minute Not a Minute?

Really, a single minute? Is being a minute late to work really that big of a deal? It can be.

First, consider Southwest Airlines (or any other airline). When does that company make money? You might say, when someone buys a ticket. Technically you would be correct. But it's really making money when the planes are in the air. If those planes sit on the ground and no one ever flies, the company doesn't make any money. So, those planes need to be in the air as much as possible. The more they are in the air, the more people are flying, and the more money Southwest makes.

Now, when does your call center make money? For many call centers, the company is making money when the customer service rep is talking to a customer. This is of course true for any sales or collections call center—if reps are not on the phone, the company is not making any money. Even for those non-revenue producing call center reps, when the phones aren't beng answered or office, you're done until your next shift. There's something to be said for that.

Another time-related advantage of working in a call center is the flexible working hours that are often available, including part-time hours and late-night shifts. This is good news for certain groups of people, such as college students and people who need that type of flexibility, such as moms or dads, who need to be at home during the day for the kids and require the opportunity to work an evening or night shift.

Another good reason for staying at your current call center position is the ability to move up. Call center work isn't always perceived as being the best place for career growth but many times the opportunity for growth and advancement does exist. During my

used, the company is not reaching business objectives such as making customers happy or getting answers to polling questions.

So, is being a few minutes late logging into the system really that big of a deal? Will the company go bankrupt if you're late for just a few minutes or if you extend your break from 15 minutes to 17? Of course not.

In fact, if you and the coworker sitting next to you both take a 17-minute break, it's really not that big of a deal. But extend that 17-minute break across hundreds or even thousands of call center representatives. Does that make a difference? Those extra two minutes times, say, 200 call center reps equals 400 minutes. That's over six-and-a-half hours of not speaking to customers. Does that make a difference to the company? You bet!

So the next time you hit that snooze button one extra time which causes you to be a few minutes late, think about the financial impact you're having on your business!

time in a call center environment, I witnessed many new people come into the company, perform well, and get promoted to higher responsibility and higher pay just months into their new job. Almost every new management position came from our frontline associates and there were some top-level executives who had been promoted five and six times, ending up as a top corporate officer. Have you seen similar career growth where you are? If so, you may consider staying.

Are there other reasons for staying?

- The pace of call center work is pretty fast. You stay busy, engaged, and have little time to get bored.
- That pace typically makes the workday go by pretty quickly.
- If you're a people person, call centers are often a great fit. From the team atmosphere to the customers on the phone, you have lots of interaction with others.

So, working in a call center is not a bad thing. In fact, it can be a very good thing!

But let's face it; many of the advantages that make call center work a good thing can also work against making this a long-term career. For example, schedules may in fact be flexible but try being late a few times and see what happens. This "can't-be-a-minute-late" issue is probably the biggest complaint I heard when I worked in a call center environment.

While you may be a people-person, talking to 70, 80, or 100 customers day in and day out can get be a little repetitious. Depending on how many of those customers yelled at you, well, that may turn you into a non-people person!

So what if, after writing the pros and cons of your current job, you decide this isn't for you? Then what?

Well, you can start by being thankful. You have a job! There are many people in this country and around the world who would jump at the chance to have your income and your benefits. Be happy that you have money coming in to pay the bills, even if just barely. This grateful attitude will make your remaining days with your current employer more fulfilling. Your grateful attitude will rub off on those around you, making it a better environment for everyone! Do not "retire in place" or "exchange hours for dollars".

Next, as you begin your job search, spend some time improving your life and work skills. There are lots of ways to improve, but three skills in particular will prepare you for success whether you find a new gig or eventually decide to stay right where you are.

These skills are easy to improve. All it takes is your conscious "choice" (there's that word again!) to improve in these areas. It's not brain surgery, doesn't require lots of math or science or any special skills or abilities. It's simply three areas of your life that, when practiced at every opportunity, will boost your current work efforts and employability!

What are they? Let's go to the next chapter.

4

Three keys to success

You look at this chapter title, "Three Keys To Success," and you're thinking one of two things:

1. "Are you kidding? I could use this! Tell me!"
2. "Yeah, sure—keys to success. Whatever."

That second response isn't surprising considering the number of references to Keys to Success in a Google search. Enter those three words and you'll get 61,900,000 suggestions. Seems like everyone has his or her own idea about how best to obtain success.

Before we explore the keys to success, we really need to define "success". We won't spend much time on this since "success" is not the primary purpose of this book. If you'd like a deeper exploration of success, check out one of the thousands of books on this topic. Yes, that's correct, thousands. In fact, Amazon offers 170,524 books on this topic!

Granted, success means different things to different people. To complicate things a bit, when defining success, some people would break that discussion into two broad areas, life success and business success.

For our purposes here, we're going to take a broader definition of success which will include your personal life as well as your business life. Why? Because the keys discussed in this book will lead to success in all areas of your life—business, family, school, relationships and just about anything else you can name.

Let's start our brief examination of success by looking at the path to success.

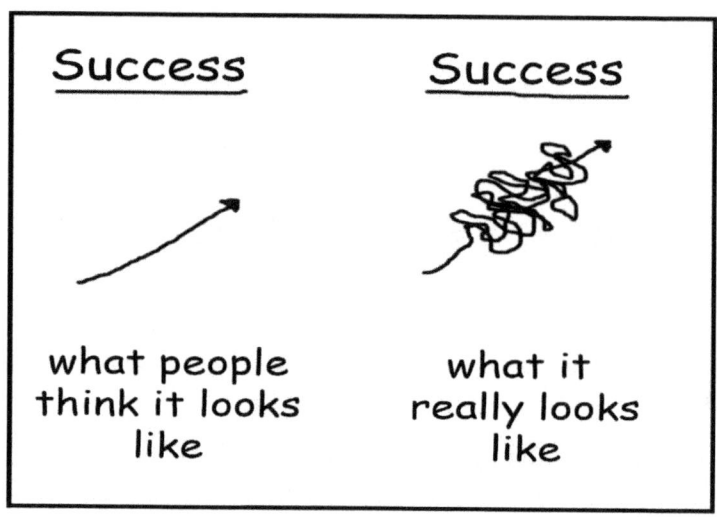

The diagram above isn't mine (sorry to the developer of this graph—I would gladly give him/her credit for the drawing if I could find the reference) but I think it's a great depiction of our path toward success. It's not a straight shot. We wish it could be. It would certainly be easier this way. But our search for success is full of ups and downs, highs and lows, advancements and setbacks.

I do have one issue with this diagram. It's not exaggerated enough. In other words, I believe life's ups are higher and the downs can be lower.

But you get the idea. While our search for success can take crazy swings including steps backwards, as long as the general trend is upward, you're moving in the right direction.

So, what is success? Well, that's up to you to define. I'm really sorry if you were looking for that "secret sauce" to success. But, I can't define success for you. Neither can any of the authors of those 170,000+ books on Amazon. Why? Because nobody knows you like you do!

Yes, your parents know you really well. So does your spouse, if you have one. Your very best friends know you very well. There are many people who can offer their opinions of success. Some may even get close to a good definition for you. In the end, though, only you can come up with the exact definition that fits your life situation. Why? Because only you know your true abilities, personality, passions, and desires, your life circumstances and your dreams.

So sorry if I got you a little excited a few paragraphs earlier. I can't tell you what success is—that's up to you.

Whatever your definition of success, there are three keys to attaining that success. Yes, there are other keys—the 7 Life-Changing Keys, 3 Keys to Entrepreneurial Success, and the 7, 8, 10, or even 20 keys to success of different kinds. Of all the available keys to success, I believe the following three are the most important:

1. Think regularly
2. Communicate well
3. Value people

Over the next few chapters, we'll review these three keys and explore how each can help you reach career (and personal) success.

Engage Your Brain!

We think every day. In fact, we think without thinking which is the exact point being made in this section! If we want to master our success then we must use the power of the amazing, most sophisticated computer in the world rather than mindlessly meander our way through this complicated world.

Make no mistake—our world is becoming more complicated with each passing day. In fact, in the late 1990s, the military invented a word to describe our world, VUCA, which stands for:

- Volatile
- Uncertain
- Complex
- Ambiguous

These four words certainly describe our world, don't you think?

How can anyone navigate such a world without engaging his or her brain, without thinking? Borrowing from Jon Acuff again, this idea of thinking, of doing things on purpose, is part of taking control of our success. "Whatever you're going to do, do it with purpose. Not as if purpose is a key you're going to find in the bottom of a trunk of old sweaters, but rather as if purpose is an approach to life that can shape everything you do."[1]

A 2010 study sponsored by IBM surveyed 1,500 CEOs from around the world and reached a similar conclusion when they identified three major global trends impacting corporations today[2]:

- The world is more complex than ever and this complexity is accelerating.

- Enterprises are not equipped to cope with this growing complexity on a global scale.

- Creative thinking is the most important leadership competency needed to navigate this increasingly complex world.

Get the picture? The world is changing, moving quickly, growing more complicated, and organizations are struggling to navigate this ever-changing environment. Keep in mind it's not only companies that must live in this VUCA world, you must also! So how do you take control of your future in such a crazy world?

The Institute For The Future, along with The University of Phoenix Research Institute, in their research report Future Work Skills 2020, says thinking is the answer. The study stated two specific types of thinking needed for career success:

1. Computational Thinking (the ability to translate vast amounts of data into abstract concepts and to understand data-based reasoning)

2. Novel & Adaptive Thinking (proficiency at thinking and coming up with solutions and responses beyond that which is rote or rule-based)[3]

Did you ever think 'thinking' was so complicated? To fully grasp the concept of "thinking", an entire book could be written (and they are!). We don't have time for that type of in-depth study here but we will spend the rest of this chapter exploring critical thinking. The idea of being deliberate in our thought, not taking the world at face value as it's presented to us, and using your mind to reach your career goals and attain some level of success as you identified above.

Let's begin our "thinking" study by finding out what you would do in the following situation.

Late one stormy, miserable night you are driving down a near-empty street when you pass by a bus stop and notice three people waiting for the bus...

1. One person waiting is an old woman, weathered and worn, dripping wet. In fact, she looks very sick.

2. Another person, to your amazement, is an old friend who once saved your life.

3. The last person is someone you've known for a while. But this isn't just any ol' someone. It's the partner of your dreams. The person you would like to spend the rest of your life with.

Your heart says you should stop on such a stormy night and give someone a ride but you realize, due to your little two-seater sports car (of course, you are very successful so can afford such a fancy car!), you can only give one person a ride.

Soooooo, who would you choose?

Tough choice, right? Before reading on, think – what would you do? The old woman certainly needs a ride, most likely straight to the hospital. But, what about the friend who saved your life years ago? While a lift out of the rain would not repay the debt you owe, it could be a down payment. And the partner of your dreams? Well, it's obvious this could be the beginning of something great!

Hmmmmmm.

It's been said this moral and ethical dilemma was actually used as part of a job application and out of 200 applicants, one answer stood out. The candidate who got the job answered:

"I would give the car keys to my friend and let him take the sick

woman straight to the hospital. I would stay behind and wait for the bus with the partner of my dreams."

What a great solution—everybody wins!

Of course, it's a little cliché-ish and not always possible to find that win/win solution. But this job applicant certainly displayed an "outside-of-the-box" thinking style.

Brain Exercises

Just like when you go to the gym to work out, in order to be an effective, critical thinker, you need to exercise your brain. So, give your brain a little workout with these questions:

- Before Mt. Everest was discovered, what was the highest mountain in the world?

- Johnny's mother had three children. The first child was named April. The second child was named May. What was the third child's name?

- In British Columbia, you cannot take a picture of a man with a wooden leg. Why not?

- A clerk at a butcher shop stands five feet ten inches tall and wears size 13 sneakers. What does he weigh?

Answers on page 127

We are constantly thinking and making decisions every day. We make hundreds if not thousands of them. Most of these decisions have little to no impact on our day or there's no right or wrong answer. It starts with questions like:

- What time should I wake up?
- What should I wear today?
- Froot Loops or granola?

Many decisions, though, can have a long-lasting impact on you or others around you and therefore require good judgment and clear, deliberate thinking.

So how does one make good decisions? Is there a process for critical thinking and one you can practice? Good questions.

Making good decisions requires two "inputs", knowledge and wisdom.

Just so we're all on the same page here, let's review a few definitions. First, knowledge: Knowledge is acquaintance with facts, figures, truths, principles—it's simply raw data or information.

Wisdom is taking all of that knowledge and putting it together for useful outcomes. Winston Churchill made a great statement that helps us clearly understand the difference between knowledge and wisdom. He said, "Knowledge is knowing a tomato is a fruit. Wisdom is not putting it in a fruit salad." How true! What would you think of someone who mixed up a nice fruit salad of grapes, cantaloupe, watermelon, and tomatoes! Yuck! Most people would say the chef was not very smart but that would be wrong. Not many people know that a tomato is actually a fruit. So this is one smart chef! So technically, you could add a tomato to a fruit salad. But it's just not a wise thing to do!

So, your brain is now in gear and you know the difference between knowledge and wisdom. So what? In other words, what does knowledge, wisdom and thinking do for you? It allows you to make good decisions, which is necessary if you're going to take control of your career. Good thinking leads to good decisions.

So how do you make those good decisions? One way is to follow the guideline below. Taking these steps can help you think critically and make your way to good decisions.

Step 1: Clearly state the problem or the decision to be made

While this seems like a no-brainer place to start, too often we run off solving problems and making decisions when we really haven't defined the exact issue at hand.

For example, do we have enough money to buy a house? Maybe you should back up and see if that's even the right living arrangement. The real issue could be where do you need to live, as in house, apartment, condo? I sometimes wonder why I'm a homeowner when changing light bulbs is about the most home repair I can do (and I've even had a bad experience here with exploding light switches and burned fingers!). So buying a house, particularly a fixer-upper, is a major decision for me. Perhaps I'd be better off in a condo or some sort of rental so someone else handles repairs and updates. So, in this case, jumping right into "can we afford this house" is not even the correct question.

While it may seem obvious, be sure to stop long enough to identify or define the problem before you begin tackling solutions. Solving the wrong problem is not only frustrating but might make your situation worse!

Okay, with the problem clearly defined, let's move to step two in the decision-making process.

Step 2: Form a strategy

Depending on the exact problem, this may be a short step or could involve multiple steps. Are there people you need to contact? Are there deadlines to be hit? Is there a particular order to solving this problem that must be followed? As with step 1, slow down enough to put a plan in place so you can make the best decision possible.

Continuing with our house example, what facts do you need to address as you are making this house-buying decision? Is your current lease up at a certain time? This could shorten your decision-making process. Have you ever purchased a house? If not, you may need to do some research on how to buy a house. How will you select your realtor? Do you need to sell your current house before buying the next one? How long are you planning to stay in your next home? All these questions and more will impact your strategy or plan. Take the time to plan well!

> "What do you want to achieve or avoid? The answers to this question are objectives. How will you go about achieving your desired results? The answer to this you can call strategy."
>
> William E. Rothschild[4]

Step 3: Collect the data

Before you can solve the issue at hand, you need to know all of the inputs and influences that impact your ultimate answer. So start your data collection. Talk to people, gathering facts, ideas, and opinions. Do some online research by "hitting that Google button on your internet machine". Be thorough during this step. This is not a spot for taking short cuts. Remember: Bad data is often worse than no data.

For our house-hunting example, this is pretty straightforward. What houses are for sale? Where are they located? What are the costs? What are the mortgage rates?

Step 4: Develop list of options/possible choices

This step takes the most time and effort. After making the list of possible solutions, you should begin "what if" scenarios, making lists of pros and cons, and putting possible solutions in a "best to worst" order.

This step also includes listing obstacles to overcome and results or consequences of each possible decision. The idea here is to anticipate and minimize those barriers that could stand in the way of successful resolution to the problem at hand.

As we continue exploring a house purchase, this may be the hardest step and may require numerous trade-offs or compromises. One house has the bigger backyard but the other house is in a much better location. One house you really like but it's a little out of your price range. Oh, the possibilities!

Step 5: Determine best option

You have the list of solutions and outcomes in front of you, so just pick the one that stands out as the best!

With all of the pros and cons listed, it's time to put those houses in order, first choice, second choice, and third.

Step 6: Implement the best solution.

Now, take action! Some people are paralyzed with certain decisions and have a hard time taking action. If you've followed this process, you have a clearly defined problem, gathered the necessary information, have a list of options and outcomes, and have the best solution in mind. So, be confident in your decision and move forward!

Go ahead—make the offer! You're close to being a homeowner!

Step 7: Evaluate outcome and decision process.

This is the step most people skip. Why? Because it takes time and this is something most people lack. Also, the decision has been made and you want to enjoy the results and move on to your next decisions. This step, however, is arguably the most important in the decision making process. Evaluation will allow you to make better decisions in the future!

Did the outcome turn out like you thought it would? Were there any steps you skipped or short-changed? How can you do a better job next time of solving a similar (or any!) problem?

If you followed steps 1-6, you most likely made a good decision and you are now enjoying your new home, the backyard, the fireplace, and your new neighborhood. While this may be the last home you purchase, maybe you'll end up buying another home someday because of a growing family or maybe a move to another city. Be sure to review your recent house-buying process. Did you like your realtor? Did you get a good mortgage rate? Is there anything you can do differently next time to make your next home purchase even better?

Don't skip this step! Evaluating the way we make decisions is just one type of self-reflection that allows us to have a continuous learning/continuous improvement mindset that is critical for our personal and professional growth. So be sure to spend some time here!

Now, you may be thinking, "Really? Who goes through all of these steps?" Very valid question.

Steps one through seven represent a very formal process that some researchers call the problem-solving cycle. It's a step-by-step guide that can be used for any question or problem.

In reality, though, must we use this formal process with each question? Probably not. For example, consider the problem of what to have for dinner.

Step 1: Clearly state problem:

Real question is: Am I even hungry?

Step 2: Easy decision so no attack strategy needed here

Step 3: Collect the data

What's in the pantry? Fridge?

Step 4: Develop list of options with consequences for each.

Salad Ingredients	Hamburger Helper	Frozen Pizza	Ice Cream
Longest to prepare	Easy to make	Quickest to make	Yummiest!
Healthy	Not really healthy	Even less healthy	Least healthy

Step 5: Determine the best option.

"I'm just going to have ice cream for dinner." (Not the best option but certainly the most fun!)

Step 6: Implement the best option

Forget the bowl, just grab a spoon and eat right out of the carton!

Step 7: Evaluate the outcome and decision process

"Hmmmm, my waistline is a bit bigger and I feel guilty. Guess I should have gone with the salad."

So those steps, while important and truly needed for some problems, make the process sound a bit more formal than is required for most decisions. Many times we simply rely on judgment:

Judgment: the ability to judge, make a decision, or form an opinion objectively, authoritatively, and wisely, especially in matters affecting action.

That's the dictionary definition. In reality, judgment is simply working through steps 1-6, sometimes even subconsciously. This is usually the case with lesser life decisions.

When minor or fast decisions are needed, most people skip a few of those formal steps or just fly through the process, simply relying on good judgment. To help make those snap or gut decisions, you need to:

Good vs. Bad

"Good judgment is what you've learned from bad judgment. Wisdom is learning from someone else's bad judgment."

Jason Young
President, LeadSmart

- Stay objective, keep your ego out of it.
- Have clear understanding of current situation.
- Have clear understanding of your limitations.
- Take a long-term approach.
- Balance risks and rewards.

Some problems or decisions, though, need a more deliberate, thoughtful process. This mental process of discovering, analyzing, and solving any particular issue takes time. So, for those larger life issues such as buying a house or how to advance your career, slow down, think, and give yourself the opportunity to come up with the best possible solution.

One last point to consider—thinking isn't just a solo act. The most effective leaders surround themselves with smart people and solicit input from them when making critical decisions. Why wouldn't we want to do the same thing?

When faced with a life question or business problem, seek others' opinions, including people outside your direct sphere of influence. These outsiders bring fresh ideas and perspective to your issue. Keep in mind—we are always smarter as a group than we are when we're alone!

Need ideas about something?
Have a **brainstorming** session!

Brainstorm by yourself or bring in others.
The more brains the better
No idea is crazy or unrealistic
Think BIG! Think DIFFERENT!
Set responses high and time low
A little pressure charges the creative juices.
When time is up, break and return for smaller session
Give your brain a break and then try again.

Your future depends on it!

Actually, the world depends on it!

"Poor leadership cripples businesses, ruins economies, destroys families, loses wars, and can bring the demise of nations. The demand for true leaders has never been greater."[5]

That's a quote from a Forbes article in late 2013. It reflects how this chapter started, saying we live in a VUCA world. What worked yesterday and how we approached problems doesn't work today. The world needs people who see and approach life differently. If we are going to solve the world's problems and "redefine the future", we need people who can think!

What about your future? Is it in a call center? Are you ready for a promotion? Is it time for a change? Whichever direction you head, make sure you think. Sometimes your decisions are no-brainers, sometimes a decision simply calls for some good judgment, and other times you'll take those practical steps to arrive at your final destination.

Call it what you want – critical thinking, think more, deliberate thought, or out-of-the-box thinking. The idea is to be deliberate in how you approach each day, each situation, and each person. Practice these "think more" insights regularly and you'll be on your way to some of the best decisions you've ever made!

5

What are you talking about?

"What we've got here is failure to communicate."

One of the most famous movie lines of all time! In *Cool Hand Luke*, the prison warden was not a kind person and after hitting his young prisoner, Luke, the warden uttered those famous words.

Failure to communicate wasn't just a problem between Luke and the prison warden; it's a struggle for everyone. Why is that? What makes effective communication so difficult and why do we regularly have miscommunication?

Because, communication involves at least two people who often have different needs and different expectations. For example, take the following sentence:

"Son, please clean up your room soon."

Pretty straight forward, don't you think? Very little room for error or misunderstanding, right? Well, let's say I said this to my son one Friday morning before I left for work. Here is what I need and expect:

Need: Aunt Gerdie is coming for the weekend and staying in your room. So, it needs to be spotless, dirty clothes picked up, and everything put in order.

Expectation: Your room will be clean by the time I get home from work and before your Aunt Gerdie arrives.

What did my son hear? Well, the exact thing I said, "Son, please clean up your room soon." But he has different needs and expectations.

Need: Time to play video games with friends.

Expectation: It's the weekend and a clean room isn't all that important.

So my son interpreted that to mean, "straighten things up, push everything into the corner or under your bed, and do this sometime over the next two or three weeks."

Different needs. Different expectations.

That's what makes effective communication so difficult. Why do I emphasize effective? Because everyone is communicating all the time, and unless we are making the effort to communicate effectively, we're likely sending and receiving wrong messages.

The 90/90 rule

Before you even say "Hello" to a new person, you're communicating. Whether being introduced to someone at a party or interviewing for a new job, you are communicating something. And in those first 90 seconds, people are making up 90% of their mind about who you are and what you're like.

Janet Elsea, in her book *The Four Minute Sell*, identifies nine characteristics of communication, three of which we are unable to control:
- Skin color
- Gender
- Age

There's absolutely nothing you can do to change these characteristics and people will make up a little bit of their mind based on these three areas. For me, I am an old white guy and there's nothing I can do to change that. I do, however, have direct control over the other characteristics Janet identifies:

- Appearance
- Facial Expression
- Eye Contact
- Body Movement
- Personal Space
- Touch

Let's say you are looking for new employment and arrive for a job interview. As the interviewer walks into the lobby, he or she is making 90% of their opinion of you when:

- He or she observes you slouched over in a lobby chair, looking half asleep.

- He or she notices you didn't "dress up" for the interview. In fact, your clothes are a little messy and your hair is out of place.

- It looks like you're angry.

- As the interviewer gets closer, you're unable to look them in the eye.

- The interviewer sticks out their hand and receives a wimpy, limp handshake.

Another characteristic?

While timeliness wasn't identified by Elsea as one of the primary communication characteristics, what message are you sending if you're late for your interview?

No words have been exchanged, yet the interviewer already has an opinion of you.

After your interview, as you are escorted back to the lobby and exchanged for the next job applicant, the interviewer is greeted by an alert-looking candidate, sitting up straight in a chair, perhaps reviewing the company's marketing material. This candidate jumps up, looks the interviewer straight in the eye, and with a smile, offers a firm handshake.

Hmmmm, who gets the job?

Granted, first impressions, although critical, are just first impressions. Given time, a wrong first impression can be turned around. Occasionally, though, such as that job interview above, you're not given that extra time.

So, before you even start communicating with words, say something about yourself. Tell people you are ready to work hard and make a difference by communicating with your dress, body movement, and your eyes. Do everything possible to make that first impression positive!

It's not just first impressions that are important. Almost everything relies on good communication:

- Learning at school.
- Listening at home.
- Convincing friends to go to the movies.

Your ability to clearly communicate directly impacts your relationships, your leadership, your job performance, and ultimately, your success. Given this fact, it makes sense that you should practice improving your communications skills.

Say What You Mean and Mean What You Say

We've all heard this before and it's certainly a good rule by which to live. However, is that the only thing you should watch, "what you say"?

Absolutely not! It's not just what you say, but how you say it! In fact, how you say things has more impact than what you actually say.

Verbal communication has three parts: gestures, words, and tone. Care to guess which one has the most impact? It's gestures. What is the second most impactful part of verbal communication? The tone you use. That means the actual words you speak are the least impactful part of your verbal communication.

Some research shows gestures to be 55% of the meaning you

are trying to communicate.[1] (these percentages are the most often quoted but not applicable to every conversation and situation). Tone accounts for another 38% of your meaning which leaves a mere 7% for the actual words you speak. If you want to be an effective communicator, you must get all three communication parts lined up.

Put Your Body Into It!

To help make your verbal communication more effective, you must get your body engaged in the conversation. Sounds a little strange, doesn't it? Consider the following ways your body can either enhance or detract from your communication.

Eye contact: This is the biggie. Eye contact or lack of it sends a number of different messages.

Can't look me in the eye when I'm speaking to you? You may be hiding something and maybe I can't trust you. Looking around the room while we're talking? I don't feel very important and you're looking for someone "better" than me.

Holding eye contact, particularly when you're listening to someone, helps you stay engaged in the conversation and shows that you are interested in the discussion.

Gestures: Using your hands, arms, and the rest of your body can enhance the conversation, making it more interesting and interactive. The meaning you're trying to convey is sometimes more easily done with proper gestures.

But remember, you can overdo it here. Too many gestures and it can become distracting, actually making your communication more difficult.

Facial expression: Closely related to eye contact is facial expression. Of course, you want to enhance your communication so something as easy as smiling is most helpful here. As you smile, perhaps nod in agreement, you are sending a friendly, positive message. People will more likely be attracted to this type of person, wanting to engage in conversation, rather than someone who sends out negative "vibes."

Posture: How you stand. Are you communicating, "Yes, I'm open to having a conversation," or are you telling people to stay away. As you speak to people, are you leaning into the conversation, engaging in the moment? Look alive!

Cell phone: What does a cell phone have to do with putting your body into the conversation? Everything! In today's society, it's too easy to push away the people in front of you while bringing those people nowhere near you right into the conversation. Stop! When you're speaking to someone (or when you're in a meeting), put the mobile phone away and be fully present in the moment. Checking your cell phone is a distraction and much like looking around the room while you're talking with someone. What you are communicating is, "I'm looking for a better conversation." Constantly looking for new text messages and Facebook updates is simply rude!

Positive and negative body language

Consider the impact that your body language has on the interpesonal communication:

- Facing your discussion partner and slightly leaning toward him/her says I'm interested in the conversation.

- Nodding your head shows engagement and understanding of the discussion.

- Arms crossed during a conversation says I'm defensive or don't like what I'm hearing.

- Hands in pockets, twisting back and forth, fidgety says you're not comfortable with the conversation. Maybe a little shy?

- Always sighing, maybe even yawning says you are bored and uninterested.

- Rolling your eyes, "This is ridiculous," and I don't believe or care for this discussion.

Gestures and body movement can enhance your communica-

The Biggest CCR Challenge

Contact center representatives have one of the most challenging jobs in the world. While performing brain surgery or flying to and from the International Space Station is extremely difficult, try connecting with someone when you've lost over 50% of your ability to communicate. That's what happens when you talk to someone over the phone—you lose the ability to send and receive messages because you can't use body language and gestures to deliver those messages.

So, for call center professionals, it's imperative to use what body language you have such as smiling and good posture. When you actually smile, it's hard to deliver a sour message. And if you're dealing with a mean or mad customer, this smiling voice will help you calm the situation and possibly turn around the customer's attitude. Sitting up straight? You're more likely to sound alert and engaged than if you're slouching way down in your chair. Keep in mind these are just the customer benefits. When your management sees you smiling and sitting up straight, they will have more confidence in your work and abilities. This positive body language will not go unnoticed!

tion. We've all seen people who "speak" with their hands. Telling stories of how they caught a football or how they fell down the steps can be visualized with good body movements, making for more effective and sometimes more entertaining communication. But don't overdo the body movement and hurt yourself or somebody else!

Bottom line? Body language and gestures can really enhance your communication. Is this basic information? For many people, yes. However, it's basic information that we need to grasp and use if we're going to be good communicators. Be aware of your body movement and gestures. Practice. Use them to your advantage. Being a good communicator is crucial if you're going to be successful where you are or where you're going.

What else conveys meaning to your verbal communication? How your words sound.

Are you a thief?

Let's examine a very simple sentence:

I did not steal your iPhone.

You can't get much more simple than that six-word sentence. Go ahead, say it out loud right now with no emotion, no emphasis on any given word (if you're in a public place, you might get some strange looks but it's okay!)

Again, pretty simply sentence, right? Well, by changing emphasis on just one word, this sentence becomes very meaningful – and could land you in jail! Or at least end a friendship.

Now, say the sentence below, emphasizing the word in bold type (again, works best if you say it out loud so you can hear it but if you're not comfortable doing this, simply say the sentence in your mind):

I did not steal your iPhone.

The sentence isn't so simple now, is it? Although the words were the same, with an emphasis on the word "I", what you're now saying is, "I know someone took your iPhone but it wasn't me."

Now, change the emphasis to "did not":

I **did not** steal your iPhone.

What are you saying here? Once again, you're saying it wasn't you, you didn't steal your friend's iPhone. This time, though, you're making sure your friend doesn't think it was you. Maybe you've said a couple of times that it wasn't you but after being accused a few times, you have to be a little more forceful in your response. What you're saying here is, "You keep accusing me but I'm telling you, it wasn't me. I did not steal your iPhone."

This time, let's emphasize the verb:

I did not **steal** your iPhone.

Here you're saying that you didn't steal the phone, you just "borrowed" it for a while. Another example of saying just one word a little bit harder and the meaning of the sentence changes completely.

Now, move on to the next word, your:

I did not steal **your** iPhone.

So now you're getting into legal problems, aren't you? You're now admitting you stole an iPhone; it just wasn't your friend's (at this point, you may start having trust issues with your friend!).

Finally, the iPhone itself. What happens when the emphasis is on this word?

I did not steal your **iPhone.**

Now, in addition to legal troubles, you've lost a friend! While you may not have stolen your friend's iPhone, you did take their watch (or wallet, or purse, or…). *

Amazing, isn't it? Just highlighting one word in a sentence with a different tone of your voice changes the meaning of the sentence completely. That's the power of tone.

What happens if you don't pay attention to this part of your verbal communication? Remember, some research says tone accounts for 38% of the meaning of what you're trying to communicate. If you're not using tone effectively, you may experience some miscommunication.

In addition to tone, there are several other verbal characteristics that impact your effectiveness as a communicator. Speech experts

* I must give credit for this section to author and motivational speaker Jason Young of BESTWORK, a business consulting organization. Jason has effectively presented this "iPhone" sentence to numerous organizations. I can't think of a better example so I use it here.

say it all starts with your breathing. Having the proper breath will allow you to have the proper speech. Sounds a little basic (or, on the other extreme, too technical) so we'll leave the first guideline at that. Just be sure you take proper breaths so you won't run out of air in mid-sentence.

Next, practice enunciating your words. This is particularly important if you spend lots of time on the phone or if you have a thick accent. If you tend to hear lots of people saying things like, "Could you repeat that please, " or "I didn't understand that," it's a good bet that you are not enunciating well enough.

The same goes for your volume. If people are constantly asking you to speak up, then you need to think about increasing your volume so you can be heard. After all, if you can't be heard, you can't be understood.

Another challenge for verbal communication, particularly for phone communication, is the pace of your speech. Not many people have the problem of speaking too slowly but many people speak so quickly that they are hard to understand or follow.

Choose the right words

In the paragraphs above, we've covered over 90% of verbal communication and how we can be more effective at communicating. We won't spend much time on that last 7% of effective communication, the actual words we choose. We'll simply look at some guidelines for choosing the right words.

Turn Off The TV!
Want to choose better words? Turn off the TV and pick up a book. In addition to increasing your vocabulary[2], reading books brings other benefits:
- Builds knowledge
- Allows you to interact/debate with others
- Improves your writing skills
- Reading fiction helps you discern emotions of others[3]
- Makes you a better leader

Probably the most impactful part of word choice is making sure your words are correct. In other words: proper grammar. Using correct grammar, both verbal and written, is key to professional success.

Unfortunately, there are several cultural trends that are working against the idea of proper grammar:

- Let's start with civility or, more accurately, incivility. According to the fourth annual Civility in America: A Nationwide Survey, 95% of respondents think we have a civility problem in America. More startling, 70% of Americans think incivility has reached crisis levels in the country. This incivility has led to a negative tone in the workplace (33% of respondents said this) and has pushed 26% of the respondents to ultimately quit their job. So we are saying ugly things to our workers and, sadly, sometimes to our customers.

- Another negative cultural trend, one that certainly contributes to this uncivil office environment, is the bad language that is often heard in the workplace. Cursing and foul language not only add to a toxic work environment but can also be career limiting. According to a 2012 CareerBuilder study, "54% of employers said that swearing made their employees appear 'less intelligent' " while 57% of the respondents said "they are less likely to promote someone who [uses] curse words."

- Technology is also pushing against good grammar. Yes, for all the good it brings us, technology does have a dark side. Tweets and texts are contributing to our inability to communicate effectively, especially through the written word. We have forgotten how to spell and how to speak in complete sentences.

- We've also forgotten how to distinguish between words such as "there," "their," and "they're," or "to," "too," and "two." Of course, this probably isn't technology's fault (were you paying attention in your high school English class?). Whatever the cause, proper punctuation and grammar are keys for most jobs and many hiring managers. This point comes into play in your written communication. When sending written communication to both customers and for your internal communications, spelling the correct word and punctuating correctly are crucial to sending the proper message.

Why do some managers put so much emphasis on good grammar? Many professionals think good grammar skills are directly related to good work ethics. Author Kyle Wiens says this:

> Grammar signifies more than just a person's ability to remember high school English. I've found that people who make fewer mistakes on a grammar test also make fewer mistakes when they are doing something completely unrelated to writing—like stocking shelves or labeling parts.[4]

To be an effective communicator, throw away the four-letter words and learn how to distinguish between two, to, and too. Better communication will help you move up the corporate ladder or change to a different corporate ladder. Either way your a winner! Uhhh, I mean "you're" a winner.

There's a lot to think about when communicating. That takes us back to the previous chapter, thinking. Too many times we simply start talking, not caring what we really say. Or, we let our emotions take over and we say something that in the end we wish we could take back. Unfortunately, when the words are out, they're out – no taking them back. So slow down a bit and be deliberate in your communication.

The Fourth Characteristic

The research we reviewed earlier in this chapter pointed out three parts of effective communication: gestures, tone, and words. I actually think a fourth part should be added.

Actions.

Have you heard the saying, "actions speak louder than words"? Well, it's not just a cliché. It could be the most important part of effective communication.

Another way to say this is with another cliché: "Do as I say, not as I do." Is this a good or bad saying? Could be either depending on how you act. Suppose, for example, you are a team leader or manager and you give a rallying cry to your followers about working hard, being on time, and doing your best. Great messages for sure!

But then the team sees you slacking off, coming in late more than a few times, and generally being lazy. What are you communicating now? Or, how can you expect your team members to keep their word if you're always apologizing for not keeping yours? In these cases, your "Let's go!" message is being drowned out by your actions.

The best communication you can give is setting a good example for others. Let your actions back up the words you are saying and there will be little chance your communication will be misunderstood.

Two vs. one

An exploration of effective communication would not be complete without a review of effective listening. In fact, logic would say we have two ears and one mouth so we should listen twice as much as we talk.

Now you may be thinking, "Really, I have to read about how to listen? I mean, come on, all you have to do is listen." Well, that is true. Listening is something that tends to come naturally. But *effective* listening? That's a different story.

Have you ever said "Good morning" to someone only to hear, "Fine, thanks" as a reply? That happened to me a few weeks ago as I was getting on an elevator at the office. The doors opened, an acquaintance walked off, and as we passed I smiled and said, "Good morning." As he quickly turned the corner and went on his way, I heard him reply, "Fine, thanks."

I didn't ask him how he was. I didn't ask him a question at all. I simply made a statement. What should have been the proper response? "Good morning" right back at me, of course!

The funny thing is this same scenario happened seconds later as I got off the elevator on the 11th floor. The doors opened and as I passed a coworker getting on the elevator, I again said, "Good morning." She replied, "Good, you?"

We may hear actual words but are you effectively hearing them? Understanding them? Offering an appropriate response? That doesn't just happen on its own. We need to work at it.

Five principles of Effective Communication:

1. Organize your thoughts in a logical manner.
2. Keep your thoughts short and simple.
3. Speak slowly enough for your audience to understand.
4. Make sure your gestures, tone, and words are sending similar messages.
5. Be a good listener.

So how do you become an effective listener? There are four things to practice:

1. Remove distractions.

We mentioned this earlier in the book. The biggest obstacle to effective listening is that smartphone you have in your hand. If you're dividing your attention between the speaker and your phone, then you aren't fully engaged in the conversation. You may miss what's being said and most likely will appear rude.

Now some of you, especially you Millennials (people born between roughly 1984 and 2000), might think this is nonsense. After all, you're good at multitasking and you see nothing wrong with talking to me and checking Facebook at the same time. While this rude behavior may simply be my opinion and the opinion of my old, "don't-understand-technology" generation, and as Millennials get older what was once thought as rude may simply become accepted behavior, science says that multitasking is actually impossible.

Do Smartphones Make Us Sad?

Comedian and actress Charlene deGuzman thinks phones may be getting in the way of real life. "It makes me sad that there are moments in our lives where we're not present because we're looking at a phone," she says.

deGuzman was so concerned about this trend that she actually takes a look at smart phone life in the video, "I Forgot My Phone" (see it at   http://www.youtube.com/watch?v=OINa46HeWg8).

Is the smart phone simply an updated Polaroid camera or video recorder? Or are we careening toward a virtual, impersonal society? Only time will tell.

For now, though, deGuzman tries to live in the moment. "I still have my phone with me, but I try to leave it in my purse. Now I find myself just taking in a moment, and I don't have to post a picture about it." [5]

According to *Financial Times* writer April Dembosky, "Our ability to pay attention and focus is also being taxed. Most studies show the human brain is not equipped to handle multiple streams of information at once."[6]

Paul Hammerness and Margaret Moore, writing for the *Harvard Business Review*, agree. "Multitasking may help us check off more things on our to-do lists. But it also makes us more prone to making mistakes, more likely to miss important information and cues, and less likely to retain information in working memory, which impairs problem solving and creativity. [7]

So, put your phone away, look me in the eye, and let's have a meaningful conversation!

2. Be aware of your non-verbal behavior.

Body gestures aren't only for when you're speaking. They are also important when you're listening. You want to use open, positive posture that makes the speaker feel at ease and assures them they are connecting with you. You can help the discussion by looking the person in the eye, smiling, and nodding in agreement.

3. Be open to what's being said.

This is a hard one. Notice it doesn't say "agree" with what's being said. It simply says be open. Suspend your judgment and listen with an unbiased, open mind. Focus on the speaker and not on yourself. Once you have a clear understanding of what the speaker is saying, you can then enter into the discussion and debate, adding your own thoughts and opinions. But if your arms are crossed in front of your chest (see #2 above) and you are not even willing to consider what's being said, then there's no way you can listen effectively. Another thing that is important here is to avoid trying to formulate your counter argument or how you wish to share your opinion while the other person is still making their point. You might miss an important part of their commentary. Always keep in mind that everybody who you come in contact with has something they can teach you. You must be open to listen to and engage with them in order to learn from them.

4. Seek to understand before seeking to be understood.

Finally, make sure you are tracking with the speaker. Again, not necessarily agreeing with what's being said, rather just making sure you understand what is being said. Don't hesitate to ask clarifying questions or paraphrase and summarize what the speaker said.

Remember, effective communication is a two-way process comprised of effective speaking and effective listening by both participants. This takes effort. If you and the person with whom you are speaking don't make that effort, the result is often confusion or misunderstanding. If you want to improve your chances of moving up in your organization or want to find another job that will help you reach your career goals, spend some time thinking about how you communicate!

6

What do you value?

During the 2013 British Open, world-famous Phil Mickelson made the above quote come alive.[2]

Phil Mickelson had just birdied the 15th hole to go 3-under on the first day of play. As he proceeded to the next tee box, Phil was greeted with applause and a chorus of "Go Phil" encouragements. As he thanked the crowd with a tip of the hat, Phil noticed a little boy sporting a cast on his left arm. Nine-year-old Ross Brown was suffering through summer with a broken arm, a cast from his hand to his elbow.

Before hitting that next tee shot in one of the biggest golf tournaments of the year, Phil walked up to the young fan, tossed him the birdie-ball from the previous hole, and said, "Here you go, little man." Phil then turned around and continued on toward the next tee box.

To Phil, giving a little boy a golf ball is nothing special. To that young boy, that little golf ball was huge!

Phil gets it.

What does Phil get? He gets people. More accurately, he understands that people matter.

Valuing people is the third skill that can separate you from the pack and have a major impact on your career. Why do people root for Phil, yell his name, and follow him across 18 holes of golf? Because they've seen Phil value people time and time again. They know Phil appreciates his fans and he shows it regularly.

Want people to follow and support you? Appreciate them. Want to grow in your career? Value people.

As we look at specific ways to appreciate people, let's briefly explore two things. Let's look at one of the life/business skills needed in 2020. We'll also take a look at ourselves.

Are you socially intelligent?

The ability to value and appreciate people starts with having social intelligence, one of ten key skills identified in the *Future Work Skills 2020.*[3]

Social Intelligence: the ability to connect to others in a deep and direct way, to sense and stimulate reactions and desired interactions.

The study states, "Socially intelligent [people] are able to quickly assess the emotions of those around them and adapt their words, tone and gestures accordingly. This has always been a key skill for workers who need to collaborate and build relationships of trust, but it is even more important as we are called on to collaborate with larger groups of people in different settings."

While you may not have heard the term Social Intelligence, you've most likely heard it using the common phrase "people skills." So the easy definition of Social Intelligence is simply interacting and getting along with other people.

Perhaps an easy way to think of good people skills is by reflecting on the Golden Rule which says: One should treat others as one would like to be treated by others. Of course, you like to be treated nicely so don't you think others like that as well? That means you should serve others and treat them with kindness. Pretty simple, isn't it? In fact, so simple we could probably move on to the next topic.

But I just can't pass up this opportunity to provide you with another list. So take a look at the following ways to improve your people skills and improve your chances at a growing, satisfying career:

Understand others

We've already talked about this, but it's probably the most important skill you can build. Knowing how people operate, their personalities, their home situations, their work, school, and family background will help you approach people in an empathetic manner. Being able to relate to others is key!

Put others first

This starts by getting over yourself. Don't take yourself too seriously. Yes, you may be a leader, in fact you may be the TOP leader of a very big organization, but don't let your ego get in the way. You're not perfect. You're not right all the time. And, most importantly, you don't know everything. Listening to others on your team is critical to the success of your group. Ask for their opinions. Getting their buy-in, getting them to take ownership, listening to their thoughts and ideas are all things a good leader does. Who wants to follow an egomaniac? Or, better put, who wants to follow a jerk?

Have empathy

Empathy is the ability to understand how someone feels, seeing things from their perspective, putting yourself in someone else's shoes. Being able to do this well will help you connect with people you are leading and your peers.

Bring people together

You're not a leader if no one is following you. Create an environment that people enjoy, where people are comfortable with you as the leader and with each other. Treat everyone as equals regardless of their job. The behind-the-scenes people are just as important (sometimes more!) as the people out in the spotlight.

Resolve conflict

Just a few sentences doesn't do conflict resolution justice but it's too important to simply ignore. Learn how to resolve conflicts quickly and thoroughly should they come up. And they will come up! Learn how to be an effective mediator and help bring the conflicting parties together to a win/win (there we go again!) resolution.

Don't be a complainer

No one likes a whiner. Need I say more? Don't get a reputation as someone who always complains. Be someone who offers up suggestions and leads with a positive attitude. Yes, everyone has to vent at some point. When this happens to you, keep your complaining short and express it only to family and close friends. But once you've vented, let it go and move on!

Have a sense of humor

OK, not everyone is funny. But at least keep it light, especially during critical moments. Don't go overboard, taking serious situations TOO lightly (or the appearance of doing so). Humor, used appropriately, disarms people and makes you an easy person to be around.

Have Manners

Most people say society is becoming more and more rude and ugly. We are lacking old-fashioned manners. According to *Harvard Business Review*, good manners allow business to function well. "Manners are the lubricating oil of an organization. It is a law of nature that two moving bodies in contact with each other create friction. This is as true for human beings as it is for inanimate objects. Manners—simple things like saying "please" and "thank you" and knowing a person's name or asking after her family—enable two people to work together whether they like each other or not."[4]

Smile

Smile a lot!!! Right along with no complaining and humor, smiling is a way to keep an upbeat attitude and atmosphere. Isn't it more pleasant to be around a smiler than a frowner?

Social intelligence and good interpersonal skills are the foundation of our third and final skill for career success, people appreciation.

2, 4, 6, 8, Who Do We Appreciate?

Did you ever say that when you were younger or yell it out as part of a cheer at a high school football game? I certainly did. That same question (minus the cheer) still applies today! What do you value and appreciate?

For me, I appreciate a lot of things:

- I appreciate a good Mexican food dinner.
- I enjoy a date night with my beautiful bride.
- I appreciate warm blankets on a cold night.
- I value time with my family.
- I appreciate someone helping me with plumbing or other house repairs.
- I enjoy chips, salsa, and a plate of sizzling fajitas.
- I appreciate a helpful answer to my credit card question.
- I appreciate the driver letting me merge onto the highway.
- I enjoy going to movies with my wife and our best friends.
- I value my mechanic when my car needs service.

As my "appreciation" list grows, I start to see a theme—most of my appreciation is directed at people. Yes, there's the occasional Mexican food dinner (as my expanding waste line shows, I enjoy chips and salsa a little too much!) and warm blanket as listed above, but most everything I have on my list revolves around people, either people close to me (family and friends) or people far away (a real person on the other end of the phone as I work through a customer service issue).

In today's computer-drenched world, it's getting harder and harder to interact with people. Sadly, many jobs are being replaced with automated systems and we are losing many human touch points and interactions. While there are many benefits to these automated systems, make no mistake, there's no substitute for that warm, friendly look, touch, or, in the case of call center representatives, voice as you interact with people.

Appreciating everyone in your life is important and, of course, this includes people in your workplace. Coworkers, bosses, people who report to you, people who serve you by keeping your computer running or bathrooms clean, they all deserve your appreciation. Let's explore some ways to appreciate the people around you at work.

Observe

We are moving so fast that we often fail to notice things, especially small things, going on around us. In fact, author Grant McCracken says one of the most under-developed soft skills is the ability to notice. Noticing that a teammate has been missing deadlines recently might point to problems in their personal life. Noticing that a normally happy, easy-going coworker has been tense and irritable lately might also point to challenges either at work or at home. And noticing the tears that are about to fall even though your team lead says all is fine should make you dig a little deeper into that answer.

Of course, if you haven't built trust with that coworker, you may never get the real story. And you may never get to know them in a deep, personal way. But if you're going to grow in your career, you must be willing to slow down, putting your own thoughts and needs to the side, and notice the people around you. Look at their facial expressions, observe their body language, and be willing to think about the meaning behind their words (note how the first two skills we reviewed, thinking and communicating, are coming into play here).

Learn

What better way to show appreciation than to put into practice the ideas and insights you gain from others. How do you learn from others? By listening to them and observing them, even pro-actively seeking their opinions and advice for your life and career challenges.

Acknowledge good work

While you're looking for real meanings behind words and facial expressions, look also for the good work being done. The kind of good work that can sometimes be overlooked in the midst of a hectic workday. Observe the people who go above and beyond their daily responsibilities and do those extra little things that bring greater success to your team and your company.

It's very easy to let people know what they do wrong. It's much harder to express what they do correctly but, the results from showing that appreciation are huge! Employees are more engaged and more satisfied. A *Harvard Business Review* article said this: "Feeling genuinely appreciated lifts people up. At the most basic level, it makes us feel safe, which is what frees us to do our best work. It's also energizing."

Showing appreciation can seem awkward or contrived but it's really not difficult. Sometimes just a simple word of thanks or encouragement is all it takes to brighten someone's day. If you want to go a little further, use the person's name and point out specifically what they did that impressed or helped you. "Jan, the way you handled that difficult customer and the patience you showed was great. I'm going to remember those answers and try them on my next customer." If you say that to Jan, she will sit up a little taller in her chair the rest of the afternoon!

Here's a crazy idea—write a note! This is becoming a lost art.

Why? Because it takes extra time and effort. It's easy to just jot down a quick "atta-boy" or "atta-girl" email, even easier to simply say thank you face-to-face. Now I'm not suggesting you ignore that face-to-face appreciation, but why not add a little extra something by taking a pen and notecard and putting some thoughts down on paper? Talk about making an impact!

Display publicly

Pulling a coworker aside and saying "Thank you" for a job well-done is great—do this as often as you can. But want to take your appreciation up a notch? Show your appreciation to everyone! Now, if you're not a manager, it may not be possible to pull your team together and make a public presentation of your appreciation. You could, though, suggest to your manager that a public "way to go" announcement is in order.

Get creative! Decorate someone's desk with balloons. Give a cookie bouquet, send a note out to the team telling about your coworker's good work, or ask your manager to throw that party!

Showing public appreciation not only boosts the confidence and attitude of your coworker, but also builds up the entire team! It creates a culture of teamwork and trust, and ultimately makes the entire team more productive.

I'm The Only Normal One Here

Now, here comes the hard part. How do you show appreciation to someone you don't really like? Sure, it's easy to appreciate people you get along with and people you like. But what about those people who drive you nuts? Well, if you work with them, if they're on your team, you can't ignore them. So, you have a choice —do you try to make the relationship work or simply keep your back toward them, offering as little interaction as possible? I think you know the correct answer.

The real question, though, is: Why don't you like them? Yes, there may be a truly mean, evil person sitting next to you and you could be justified in not liking that person. Most likely, though, that person isn't mean or evil, they are just different than you.

I learned this lesson when my family moved to Bulgaria and I became the headmaster of a small school. As soon as we exited the plane in Sofia, Bulgaria's capital, my entire family started saying things like, "That's weird," or, "That's not how you do this." We said statements like that over and over and over. We soon realized, however, that those things, those customs, those ways of doing life really weren't weird, they were just different. Changing our language and our mindset from "That's weird" to 'That's different" allowed us to appreciate our new surroundings, including the Bulgarian people.

This mind shift is needed at work if you're going to appreciate everyone, both the people you like and the ones that might rub you the wrong way. Before you can start looking at others, though, you need to do a quick self-assessment.

Why start with you? Well, before you can understand others you need to understand yourself. I'm not talking about spending lots of time and money figuring out who you are through one of those deep, corporate self-discovery tools (although if you ever have the chance to take a self-assessment such as this, do it—they can give you great insight into how and why you act and think in certain ways).

For our purposes here, we're just talking about being aware of your likes and dislikes. For example, take out a pen or pencil and place a mark where it best describes you on the following scales:

Introvert .... Extrovert

Quick Decisions .... Analyze

Loud..Soft Spoken

Funny..Serious

Humble ....Prideful

Easily Irritated..Long Fuse

That wasn't a hard exercise, was it? What is hard, however, is getting along with people who are different than you. So you're quiet. Do you want to hang out with someone who is loud all the time? Of course not. Same for funny and serious. If you're a comedian and always the life of the party, you probably don't like hanging out with people who don't share your sense of humor.

You would rather hang around people who are like you. That's understandable. People who are different than you tend to drive you crazy. But guess what? You drive them crazy! While you would rather not hang out with that always-serious person, they would agree. In other words, they don't necessarily want to hang out with you!

So when we pick our friends and how we spend our free time, we tend to hang out with people like us. Unfortunately, we don't get to choose our co-workers so we're working right next to people who just might drive us nuts!

Whatever the reason (and being loud or quiet isn't really a reason at all!) your coworker rubs you the wrong way, decide to overlook it. It's a simple decision. I didn't say easy, but it is simple.

Now that you're overlooking the negative, focus on the positive. What is it that stands out about the person? Everyone has positive qualities that can be praised and emulated. Everyone. What is it about this person that can be appreciated? Works hard under pressure? Always on time? Always helpful? Always has a smile? What?

That's where the good people skills that we explored earlier come into play. You may be a "people-person", someone who gets along with everyone and likes to be around people all of the time. On the other hand, you may need to work on your people skills a bit and that's okay. You're in good company. Just about everyone needs to work on some aspect of their people skills. The good news is that people skills can be learned, practiced, and improved. It does, however, take time and focus.

The Bottom Line

People matter.

People need to be appreciated.

Generous amounts of appreciation and praise will motivate individuals and improve teams. Appreciation and praise will help both your professional and personal life by bringing people together, lifting their spirits, making people feel noticed.

It is also one of the keys to your professional growth. Your boss, your teammates, people who work for you, people across the company that only occasionally cross your path and even your customers, all deserve to be thanked, praised, and appreciated.

Try it! Thank someone...........today! Take out a pen and paper and write out a note of thanks to someone who has made a difference in your life or who has done something special today. Go on......do it now. Or, perhaps you could appreciate someone with a cookie or a balloon. Trust me, you won't be disappointed.

7

It's time to answer some questions

Before we move forward, let's take a look back. What have we studied during the first half of this book?

To start, we explored how you've ended up where you are today. You might be a Customer Service Representative. You may be deep in the back office of a large corporation, paying company invoices day in and day out. Maybe you are on a small team late at night, quietly cleaning up an entire building long after all of the other workers have gone home. Regardless of where you are at this point in time, you probably didn't dream of doing this when you were five, six, ten years old.

If you think your work is meaningless, think again. "Every calling is great when greatly pursued," said author and poet Oliver Wendell Holmes.[1] Whatever you do, as long as you do your best, your work is worthwhile. It has meaning.

Keep in mind that, at the end of the day, you are not a collector, clerk, janitor, or jailer. You are a People Improvement Specialist. In some way, your job touches people and you can either do that well, improving their lives, or you can take a "this doesn't matter" approach, leaving the other person wanting more. Never forget that whatever you do, you, and your work are important.

We also reviewed three life skills that, when performed well, will help you advance your career either with your current employer or by preparing you for that next professional step. Those life skills are:

Think!

Be a better communicator.

Value people.

That's it! Three incredibly important life skills. Do these well and your life situation will improve.

Are you still with me? Hope so! Of course, it's your choice to either keep reading or take a pass on investing the short amount of time needed to improve your current career. Trust me (do you trust people who say "Trust me"?), the ideas and steps in this book work. I've seen it in my life and in the lives of countless others. And here's the crazy part—there's really nothing new in this book. There are no new ideas on how to be successful in business or in life. And don't believe anyone who claims to have that new idea!

Even though this book is full of tried-and-true ideas, there's still a problem—we often forget the basics. We forget or just plain ignore the essential things that have made successful careers for years. We all need to back up from time to time, review our work situation, and plan our next steps.

Author and speaker Rick Rigsby wrote a great blog entry titled *Living On Purpose*.[2] I love that title—*Living On Purpose*. It can be applied to our lives in so many ways including our work situation. In fact, we can probably adapt that title for our use here, "Working On Purpose."

Think about it. Here you are, grinding it out day after day after day. Then you pick up this book and I've asked you to do three things: think more, communicate better and value more. Now what? Maybe you're saying to yourself, "I'm cool with these three life skills. I'll think more, communicate better, and value people around me. Isn't that enough?" Well, no, it's not.

Of course, if you think, communicate, and value more, you will start down a path to a better tomorrow. So start thinking, communicating, and valuing!

But if you want your career to really take off, I mean go to a completely different level or even a different direction, you need to begin working on purpose. How do you work on purpose? By asking yourself four simple questions.

Yes, there are lots of lists out there as a quick Google search will confirm.

Ten Questions to Live Your By

Six Powerful Questions That Will Change Your Life Forever!

35 Questions That Will Change Your Life

I believe, however, 35, 10, and even 6 questions are too many. I think you can improve your life with just four simple questions. In fact, I'm going to make it even easier on you. I'm going to give you the answers!

YES!

That's it! Yes! That simple answer to these four simple questions could take your career to a new level, in a different direction, or both. And that is certainly less complicated than 35 different answers to 35 different questions! Want to know more? Read on.

Going Back To School

As I write this book, two of my three boys have recently started a new school year (my oldest is already out of college). Do you remember those days? UGH! That first day and that first week were the worst. All I could think about was the fact that we had another nine months of school, nine months of learning. And I actually liked school! But it was still school. It was the end of late nights, sleeping in, playing baseball, and playing kick-the-can (you young people reading this book may not know what that is – just hit the Google button on your internet machine again to find out).

If you're going to be professionally successful either where you are today or, more importantly, where you want to be tomorrow, you must go back to school. Well, you don't have to actually go back to school. You must, however, be willing to answer yes to our first of four questions:*

Am I willing to be a continuous learner?

It's no secret the world is moving quickly. Earlier in this book we looked at the term VUCA which stands for volatile, uncertain, complex, and ambiguous. That certainly describes our world.

Things are changing all around us all the time. Did you ever have to play outside with just a stick or, even "worse", just your imagination? I did and that was just 40 years ago. Today's kids? They don't need an imagination because the wireless controller in their hands allows them to play a very realistic-looking game of soccer or football.

Speaking of wireless……….. actually, wires…………. do you remember when telephones had a wire coming out of them and running into the wall? If you're a Millennial, you may not have experienced this. We've gone from those old landlines to small, portable, dumb phones to phones that are rarely used for talking but can help us find the trendiest night spot, guide us there through navigation, and chronicle the entire night by taking pictures and posting them to the web for all the world to see.

In the business world, change is also happening at an ever-increasing rate. According to the *Future Work Skills 2020* research,

* **NOTE:** I must give credit to these four questions to author and radio personality Dennis Prager. While listening to his radio show one day, I heard him say these four questions with regard to success. While I am repeating last three questions, his first question was, "Are you willing to think or use common sense?" Since we discussed critical thinking as one of the skills needed for success, I have substituted being a continual learner as our first question. Thank you for the inspiration, Mr. Prager!

Transdisciplinarity and Cognitive Load Management will be two of the top 10 skills needed in business.[3] Transdisciplinarity? I'm not even sure that was a word just a few years ago!

> Transdisciplinarity: literacy in and ability to understand concepts across multiple disciplines.

> Cognitive Load Management: ability to discriminate and filter information for importance, and to understand how to maximize cognitive functioning using a variety of tools and techniques.

How will you prepare for this rapidly approaching and constantly changing future? Well, you don't really need to go back to school (although there's nothing wrong with that!). No, you will prepare yourself for your future and for your career path by being a continual learner. You must be willing to learn new skills such as these and adapt to new, changing work environments. This is certainly a challenge as a *Harvard Business Review* article stated in an article in early 2012: "Are You Learning as Fast as the World Is Changing?"[4]

The last sentence of the article's first paragraph says it all:

> "In a world that never stops changing, great leaders never stop learning."

This statement isn't just for leaders; it's for everyone. If you want to work on purpose and improve your current situation, you must be willing to put some effort into your career. Not just a little effort but some honest, hard work. That means learning new things and keeping up with the changes going on all around you. The HBR article went on to point out three ways to be a continual learner. Called "habits of the mind", these three abilities are crucial if you want to grow and thrive in our ever-changing world.

First, learners must have a wide field of vision. In discussing this point, the HBR article pointed to Steve Jobs and the original Macintosh computer. Even though it was a computer full of semiconductors and software, Jobs spent more time talking about other things like art and music. In other words, to know about computers, Jobs had to know about a wide range of other things.

So if you want to be better at what you currently do or want to take your career someplace else, start looking around. Be observant. Start looking for people, experiences and ideas outside of your current field of vision. "If you want to learn faster, look and live more broadly," HBR concludes.

Second, the best way to get new ideas for your current or next job is to look for tried and true ideas in areas outside of your current field. The article mentioned Lexus engineers looking to Apple (computers) and Four Seasons (hotels) for inspiration. HBR also pointed to London's Great Ormond Street Hospital and how its doctors and administrators redesigned their surgical procedures after reviewing how Ferrari's Formula One team performed their pit stops.

If you're in Customer Service in, say, a bank or a manufacturer, can you learn any-thing about great customer service from your regular trips to Starbucks?

> **If you are not willing to learn, no one can help you. If you are determined to learn, no one can stop you.**
> **Author unknown**

And, number three, continual learners are not loners. This might be a little difficult for you introverts but if you want to learn all the time, be with people. All kinds of people, particularly people who are different from you. It's easy to hang out with people like us. In fact, that's what friendship is all about, right? Who surrounds themselves with "friends" who have different ideas of entertainment, have different personalities, and love foods we hate?

Often, new ideas, new ways of thinking, and new opportunities come from people outside our immediate sphere of influence. So, the bigger circle of people you know, the more learning you are likely to do.

> **I have never met a man so ignorant that I could not learn something from him.**
> **Galileo**

By the way, you can learn from people you barely know or people you meet. On most days, you come into contact with dozens or even hundreds of people, at work, of course, and family members. But what about people on the train or in the grocery store. Some of us stand in long lines at Starbucks, waiting for that double mocha frappa with a shotta something. How about making a connection while inching up to the counter? Rather than staying to yourself, head down while staring at your smart phone, why not strike up a conversation with the person next to you? Who knows where a conversation will go after a simple smile and hello (in addition to making the wait just a bit brighter!).

The point is this. We need knowledge, data and facts, which today's technology puts at our fingertips. However, it's through people that we find most of our opportunities in life. So, in addition to living on purpose and working on purpose, try seeking people on purpose.

> You can learn from anyone. Start up a conversation whenever possible. We can keep to ourselves, or say hello with a smile and meet someone, and maybe even learn from them.
>
> Dave Kerpen
> CEO, Likeable Local,
> Author & Speaker

Those three points from *Harvard Business Review* are a great start to our exploration of continuous learning. There are several more characteristics of life-long learners that are critical for a successful career. Let's explore those now:

They listen more than they talk.

Don't be afraid to speak up, offer your opinion. But be sure to listen to all the opinions around you and don't be too quick to jump into the conversation.

They ask lots of questions.

This is especially true if you don't understand something. Don't pretend you know or understand something when you don't! There's nothing wrong with asking basic questions. That's the point! That's how you learn! If you do pretend, you may get caught in an embarrassing situation. And if you have a question, chances are someone else is asking the same thing!

They surround themselves with other continual learners.

None of us is as smart as all of us put together. Continual learners push each other to learn even more.

They are observant.

Look around; see what's going on around you. You can pick up ideas in the smallest thing.

For example, I regularly teach customer service. As I was sitting in a Starbucks one day, a company that prides itself on offering superior customer service, I saw a barista take the best parking spot right in front of the door. This barista walked in and started her shift. Leaving that spot for a customer would have been great customer service. A small thing I noticed that I will use next time I teach.

They know their strengths and weaknesses.

Know what you do well, and know the areas that are challenging for you. There is much written about which strategy is more productive, concentrating on your strengths or weaknesses. To fully explore this area would take at least another chapter or two if not an entire book (of which there are many). The general consensus seems to be working on your strengths is more productive. Your strengths will always be what allow you to move forward and your weaknesses will always hold you back. So be aware of your weaknesses and work around them when necessary.

For example, if you have the opportunity to build a team or hire someone who will work for or with you, try to find someone who is strong in an area where you are weak. You may also have to turn down some opportunities that depend on abilities or characteristics that are your weak spots.

On the other hand, know your strengths and work to develop them. You will get "more bang for your buck" with this strategy and will ultimately reach new career highs and be happier in the process.

They ask for honest feedback from coworkers and managers.

Yikes! This is hard for most people. No one likes to hear criticism. If, however, you want to be a continuous learner and change your current career circumstances, getting outside opinions from people you trust will help you focus your personal improvement activities and may help you see some blind spots that you didn't even know were there (that's why they're called blind spots!). Remember feedback is a gift!

Feedback vs. Criticism

Providing and (especially) hearing negative feedback can be difficult but it's critically important for career and personal success. Be careful, though, not to cross over the line to criticism!

Feedback	Criticism
Concrete information	Judgmental, accusatory
Avoids speculation	Negative assumptions
Specific behaviors	General, void of details
Precise	Tends to exaggerate
Calm, low-key	Emotional
Helps, supports	Pressures, attacks

They are curious.

What do you wonder about? Do you wish you knew and understood how certain things work? What was life like in the past and what might it look like in the future? Being curious will help your career aspirations. How? Because as you act on your curiosity by searching for answers, your mind and horizons will expand. You'll find yourself having new conversations with new people. And you never know where those conversations will lead you!

They are flexible and adaptable.

Don't be afraid to change and try new things. Don't be that person who says, "We've always done it this way."

Finally, as a continuous learner, you are always looking for new ways to learn. Earlier in this chapter, a section was titled "Going Back To School". It was meant to be a little tongue-in-cheek but then again maybe not. What's wrong with going back to school? Maybe take some night classes? Yes, your schedule is already packed but maybe taking one night a week for the next several semesters or even years can put you in a position to take a big step in your career.

Join a MOOC

Want to go to school but don't have the funds? Try taking courses through a Massive Open Online Course, known as a MOOC. These are courses offered on a large scale and are free to access via the internet. These courses are similar to university courses and, in many cases, are actually offered by the universities themselves.

Major universities such as MIT, Stanford, Harvard, and Yale offer their degree material free of charge to anyone. You don't even have to be accepted by the school.

Of course, the downside is you won't walk away with the actual degree even though you may have passed every required course. The upside? You'll have the knowledge! And perhaps you can turn this knowledge into a new, exciting career!

It might not be school you attend but maybe a course or training opportunity that your company offers. Many organizations have training programs, some led by facilitators and many programs offered online. If your company offers training, take full advantage of these opportunities!

In addition to career advancement or enhancement, continuous learning offers another great benefit—you never get burned out.

Notice I didn't say tired or even exhausted, I said burned out. Of course there will be times in life when you are physically and mentally tired. Working overtime and then stopping at the store as you race home to prepare dinner for the family? Those are tiring days for sure.

Being a continual learner, however, helps you push through those tiring days or even weeks and months. Always looking for new information, new ways of doing things, new skills, and new people to meet gives you energy and keeps you from hitting the burnout or checkout buttons.

Ron Shaich, founder and CEO of Panera Bread noticed this even in the midst of eighty-hour workweeks.

"Thankfully, I've never experienced the chronic exhaustion, inertia, frustration, and cynicism that come with a temporary slump or even classic burnout. Hence, I've never had reason to refresh my spirit and renew my spark.

The reason, I think, is that I view my work as a lifelong learning journey. I go to work to learn about how the world works. How humanity works. And what will work in the world.

I'm not a scientist. We don't cure cancer at Panera. We don't launch shuttles into space. But we do touch the lives of 8 million people each week in thousands of cafes across the country.

If you find meaning in your work and you go to work to learn about life, I doubt you'll ever have reason to recharge. The work itself will renew you."[5]

So, do you want to keep your energy high and burnout level low? Look for ways to learn – constantly!

Here are some practical ideas for
being a continual learner.

Find a mentor: More than just about any other activity, asking someone to be your career coach will supercharge your career success. But you can't ask just anyone. The friend in the cubicle next to you? He or she may be in the same boat you are! So ask someone who has "been there, done that", someone who has already enjoyed a level of career success. Of course, this needs to be someone you trust, as this person will most likely speak some truth into your life that is sometimes hard to hear.

Read: According to the *Harvard Business Review*, ". . . deep, broad reading habits are often a defining characteristic of our greatest leaders and can catalyze insight, innovation, empathy, and personal effectiveness." The article went on to say, "Evidence suggests reading can improve intelligence and lead to innovation and insight."[6]

Go to lectures: A quick Google search for "Lectures Dallas Fort Worth" resulted in 15 possibilities in the next month (I actually just registered for a leadership lecture at a local chamber of commerce!). Hearing speakers of any kind – authors, artists, business professionals, politicians, just about anyone – is a chance to expand your knowledge. Another benefit? Maybe you will meet someone at the lecture who can help you in your career journey!

Watch good TV: I'm not saying put a complete end to your reality show watching ways. I am saying to add a little educational entrée to your TV diet. Using my Netflix account, I have access to hundreds of documentaries.

Webinars: Improve your professional skills using webinars. Many webinars are free and most are hour-long sessions.

Current events: What's going on in the world? How about your state, city, or even neighborhood? Watching and reading the news allows you to build your depth of knowledge and enter into intelligent discussions with others.

Company opportunities: Does your company offer training? Maybe some online courses? If so, take advantage of those opportunities! Ask your manager how you can become active in your company's educational offerings. Ask also about company functions you can attend. For example, is your CEO speaking somewhere local? Perhaps you can attend the presentation.

Take control

Change is all around us, and the pace of change is accelerating. Ideas and products that were invented just two or three years ago are already outdated or even totally obsolete. We can't even think of the problems we'll be solving two or three years from now.

If you want to improve your chances at a successful, satisfying professional life, you simply can't stand still while change takes place all around you. To avoid being left behind, you must take control of your learning. Be deliberate in changing your current circumstances by being a continuous learner as described above.

Are those a lot of steps? Yes.

Do continuous learners need to do all of those things? Yes, all of those activities are beneficial.

Can you really do all of those things? Yes, I believe you can.

So, that's question #1—Am I willing to be a continuous learner? Answering yes to this question is the first step to a brighter and more satisfying professional career.

One down, three to go. Ready for the second question? Okay, read on!

8

Question #2

I realize everything we've examined so far may not be easy, especially if your life is already maxed out. Full time job, maybe two. Single parents doing work and making sure the kids get their work done as well. Paying bills. Getting the car repaired. LIFE!

None of the concepts are particularly difficult or hard to understand. But they may add pressure to an already pressurized life. What are the rewards for choosing to push through with these concepts?? As Visa would say in their commercials – PRICELESS! Are you still with me? I hope so!

Question #1: Am I willing to be a continuous learner?

Answer 'Yes' with enthusiasm!

Question #2:

Am I willing to work hard?

Here again, if you want to better your life and the life of your family, the answer is yes. Let's explore this in the next few pages.

This question, while easy to answer, is in some ways the most difficult. Why? Because some people reading this book may already see themself as working hard. Single parents, families that juggle the kids as both parents work, and people working two jobs – aren't you already working hard? Most likely, yes. "And you want me to work harder?" you might be thinking.

Well, let's put it this way. Regardless of how hard you are currently working, if you are not satisfied with your current job, you need to do something different. I'm willing to bet that for most readers this means working harder.

For some readers, though, it might mean one of two things, either working smarter or making different choices.

Smart Working

I'm a little hesitant to use the "work smarter" line which is a popular concept today. By saying this, I'm implying that what you're currently doing is dumb. That's not the intended message. Perhaps a better term to use is efficient working.

Let's not confuse hard work with being busy. Some people are moving constantly from one task to another, "working hard." At the end of the day, though, there could still be a nagging feeling of a lack of accomplishment or progress. Maybe changing the way you work, working more efficiently or "smarter", can help. If this rings true for you, try changing your days with some of the following tips:

Remove distractions: For most people, work is interrupted by constant distractions. Phone calls, checking Facebook, running to the vending machine for a snack, sending a text message every 10 minutes, having someone stop by your desk to talk about last night, checking Facebook again—the number and types of distractions seem endless. To allow more concentrated efforts on your work at hand, try removing as many distractions as possible. For me, that meant removing all the little games from my iPhone. Yes, I had Angry Birds on my phone and I didn't play it often. But ten minutes here plus another 3 minutes playing Words With Friends began to add up. So I removed these distractions by removing these apps from my phone. A hard choice, yes, but it made me a more productive worker. How can you remove distractions from your day, thus becoming a "smarter" worker?

Concentrate: You've already helped yourself concentrate by removing distractions. Take it a step further by cutting back on your multitasking. Although many people say they can multitask, they really can't unless it's something that doesn't take brainpower such as cleaning the dishes and talking on the phone at the same time. But if you need to pay attention or learn something, you need to concentrate. Blogger Douglas Merrill said, "When you're trying to accomplish two dissimilar tasks, each one requiring some level of consideration and attention, multitasking falls apart. Your brain just can't take in . . . When information doesn't make it into short-term memory, it can't be transferred into long-term memory for recall later. [Multitasking is] making you less efficient, not more."[1]

Plan Your Day: Do you put actual thought into how you spend your day or week? Time management will help you reach your goals and do so with less stress. Manage your time using a day planner or some sort of scheduler. Online, your smart phone, pen and paper – whatever works best for you. Plan time for work, grocery shopping, time with the family, workouts (if you're not healthy, it will be hard to get things done). Plan EVERYTHING! Effectively using this skill and these tools will make you a master of your schedule, lower your stress levels, and help you keep track of and complete projects. All of this PLUS it makes life more fun!

Prioritize: Do you make To Do lists? Do your notes simply list all your "To Do" items in no particular order? How do you know what to do and when to do it? Closely related to planning your day, prioritizing the important things will make you more effective and less stressed. We all have more to do than time to do it in so we must prioritize our work. What items are critical or time sensitive? Be sure to get those done first!

NOTE: Prioritizing your day/work/life means sometimes you will be forced to say no. In fact, the inability to say no is one of my weaknesses. I hate to disappoint people and don't like saying no. So too often I say yes, accepting assignments and invitations and then realize I'm doing too much and doing none of it well. You may even have to say no to good things! In the long run, though, you will be more productive, more reliable, and more satisfied.

Don't Procrastinate: Don't put off until tomorrow what can be done today. Many times we delay doing something just because we can. It's not due right now. Or tomorrow. Or even next week. So we have time, right? Well, if we "wait until tomorrow" too many times, we'll run out of tomorrows. And then we'll find ourselves scrambling to complete a project. The result? We're either late or the finished product is less than our best.

Different Choices

Choices. This word keeps popping up, doesn't it? Every time we've used the word it requires you to act. You must make a choice. There's no fence riding, no choosing not to make a choice. In other words, not making a choice is a choice itself!

For those of you who already have full schedules, you may be saying, "There's no way I can work harder!" Okay, that may be true. But if you want to change your work circumstances, something has to change, right? That's where choice comes into play.

You may have to make some adjustments to your life. You may have to choose to stop doing some things in order to concentrate on a different area of your life. Even if your life is full of "good" things—volunteering, church activities, playing on your company's softball team—if you're going to make time for continual learning or find a way to invest in your career, you have to give something up from your already-full schedule. So, it's not just a choice you need to make, it's a really hard choice!

We won't spend much time here so I'll simply ask you to review how you're spending your time. All of it. Don't guess. Don't say to yourself, "Oh, I probably spend about 20 minutes a day on Facebook." If you're a pretty regular user, chances are you spend more than 20 minutes a day.

Rather than guess, spend a week tracking your time. Track everything. How much time you spend preparing food and actually eating. How much time do you work out or exercise? How much time getting ready for work, driving or commuting to work, working, and then returning home.

If you're like me, this is a hard exercise because I'm not a detail-oriented person. But if I'm going to get a handle on how I spend my time so I can make those difficult choices, I need to know where all of my time goes. I'm talking the two minutes here checking scores on ESPN, the five minutes I take to pick up around the house, and the fifteen or twenty minutes I spend walking the dog.

Do this for a week. No cheating! Don't back off your Facebook or Call of Duty time just so it doesn't show up on your weekly schedule.

Armed with a week's worth of daily activities, you're ready to make some decisions. How much time did you spend on Facebook, Xbox, or any other chill-time activities? Can you give up some time here, switching over to some sort of career investment activities?

Remember, you only have 24 hours in a day and you need to make time for sleeping, (get plenty of rest if you want to operate at your best every day) eating, (a good diet is also important to a good career) and fitness (relieves stress, improves focus).

That's it for wise choices. Even with an already-full life, you can still find a way to invest in yourself and your future.

Let's continue our exploration Question #2, Am I Willing To Work Hard, by reading about 18-year-old Jhaqueil Reagan. His story begins before he's actually working.

As Jhaqueil was walking one snowy, February morning, he stopped Art Bouvier to ask how much further it was to his final destination. After Art told him it was another six or seven miles, Jhaqueil said thanks and continued walking.

About fifteen minutes later, Art, owner of Papa Roux Po Boys and Cajun Food in Indianapolis, was driving with his wife when he spotted Jhaqueil still walking. Art pulled over, spoke to Jhaqueil, and learned he was planning to walk ten miles for a job interview. Did you get that? This young man is **walking ten miles** just to interview for a job!

Art told a local TV station, "I'm thinking to myself, here's a kid walking almost 10 miles in the ice and slush and snow for the hope of a job at minimum wage. That's the kind of story my parents used to tell, 'I used to walk 5 miles in the snow, to and from school and it was up hill both ways.'"

Jhaqueil was forced to quit high school at 16 when his mother died. While taking care of his siblings, he earned his GED. Talk about a hard choice! Complete high school or take care of your brothers and sisters? Wow!

After slogging through the ten-mile snow trek, Jhaqueil was told the job had already been filled. Fortunately, Jhaqueil had flagged down Art to ask how much further he had to walk. As a result of that encounter, Art hired Jhaqueil to work at Papa Roux. "It's been a while since I've met someone so young with a work ethic like that!" Art commented.

> Every time you stay out late; every time you sleep in; every time you miss a workout; every time you don't give 100% – You make it that much easier for me to beat you.
>
> Unknown[2]

"I tell every single applicant, I can show you the ropes, but what I can't teach is work ethic. Show up. Be on time." Art was also impressed when he saw Jhaqueil walking to his interview two hours before the scheduled time just so he wouldn't be late.[3]

Work ethic. The key to answering "yes" to this chapter's primary question, "Am I willing to work hard?" As Art states above, a strong work ethic can't be taught. We can teach things like leadership, computer skills, and life skills such as communication and critical thinking which this book has attempted to do. For work ethic, though, it's something you have to choose (there goes that word again!). Jhaqueil understood that if he wanted to change his life situation, he had to wake up early and start walking just for the chance to work!

While I can't teach or make you have a strong work ethic, there are some things you can concentrate on and practice that will help drive you to that strong work ethic.

Character

There is no way we can do this word justice in the next few paragraphs. Entire books, hundreds of them, have been written about this topic, but we can't discuss work ethic without mentioning and briefly reviewing this topic.

In his book *UnCommon*, former Indianapolis Colts head coach Tony Dungy gives us two great definitions of character:[4]

#1. "Outwardly, character reflects an inner life committed to honor and uncompromising integrity."

and

#2. "Character is the sum of everything you are: your values, your actions, your words, and your thoughts."

Dungy writes, "Character begins with the little things in life. I must show that I can be trusted with each and every thing, no matter how trivial it may seem." He continues by saying—and this is key—"Over time, we create ourselves and build our character through the little acts we do."

When discussing character, you'll hear related words such as integrity, ethics, morals, and honesty. All slightly different and worthy of exploring further (in fact, when you finish this book, why don't you continue studying this topic by reading Dungy's book or another book on character?).

Character and integrity extend to all aspects of your work life and impact relationships with your coworkers, your supervisors, and your customers. So, as you work on building a strong work ethic, start by building a strong character!

Attitude

Is the glass half full or half empty? "Attitude is everything" some people say. Well, it may not be everything but it's a big part! More about this is the next chapter.

Timeliness

First, don't procrastinate. This was mentioned earlier. Have a "Do it now" approach and don't delay your work.

Second, be on time. Not only does being on time help with your overall time management but also it shows respect for others. Punctuality is key to a strong work ethic.

Third, hit your deadlines. Related to the idea of being on time above, make sure you do what you said you would do when you said you would do it. Did you follow that? Stated differently, be a man or woman of your word. If you say you will call tomorrow at 2:00 p.m., then call at 2! If you agreed to provide your boss a report by the end of the week, be sure you manage your time in order to provide that report by the end of the week.

Related to this "be on time" idea (and related to clear communication that we explored earlier), be sure to clearly define your deadlines. If you are in a position to set a deadline, set the expectation clearly and ask for understanding. If you are on the receiving end of a deadline, ask questions to clarify any ambiguous language.

For example, what does "end of the week" mean? Is that any time on Friday? Is it 5pm on Friday? How about Sunday at midnight? If you are not certain about a deadline, ask some questions. You can't hit a deadline if you don't know what it is!

Accountability

Be responsible for your work and own up to your mistakes. We just read about the importance of hitting deadlines. Does this mean you will hit every one for the rest of your life? Probably not. So when you do miss a deadline or make some other mistake, own it and communicate it as early as possible. Apologize for it.

Correct the problem, and learn from it—how can you avoid this mistake in the future?

Related to this idea is the sense of teamwork. When you are working on a team, be sure to have a "we're all in this together" attitude. This means pitching in and helping others with their work even if it's not your area of responsibility. When your coworker succeeds, so do you and everyone else!

Quality

Finally, make sure the work you produce is good work. Notice I didn't say perfect although there's nothing wrong with shooting for that goal. Want to move up from your current position? Make sure the work you do today is quality stuff. Want to be known as someone who is dependable and helpful? Take the extra steps to deliver work, advice, and information that is timely, accurate and dependable. Don't let sloppy work keep you from having a strong work ethic.

Are you getting the idea that hard work is important? It's actually what separates good from great or successful from unsuccessful. Here's the good news—it's something everyone can do! Yes, having knowledge and skill in certain areas is important, but the key to making the most of that knowledge and those skills is your overall effort. In other words, hard work.

What's the payoff? Well, as we've suggested several times throughout this book, the payoff may be a different job for you. It might be a promotion where you are, a new job with another company or even a completely different life direction. In the end, you'll probably have more money and, more importantly, greater satisfaction with your life situation.

While more money is certainly a good thing, that self-satisfaction, knowing you've done your best, is probably the most rewarding of all. Jon Gordon, author of *Training Camp: What the Best Do Better Than Everyone Else*, believes hard work is noticed and rewarded:

"I have found that when you work hard, people notice. Maybe not right away, but eventually people notice, and rewards happen without you pushing for them. They naturally come your way.

The key is to do your best every day and strive for excellence in all that you do. If you are working hard and looking for the reward, this usually creates a neediness that stops others from rewarding you. Rewards come to those who are humble and hungry—humble in that you are striving to learn, grow and improve every day, and hungry with a passion to be your best and bring out the best in others.

When you make excellence your focus, success and rewards are just a nice byproduct. The reward is in the work, not in the outcome."[5]

Read that last paragraph again. It is so important! In fact, those two sentences could be the review of this entire chapter! In other words, committing to and doing our best work and then feeling good about that work is all we need!

Do you get the idea that hard work is key if you want to get ahead in life or get ahead of the competition that is applying for that same promotion or same job? Yes, there are a number of things we've discussed in this chapter—working more efficiently, being dependable, having character, being on time—that go into the pot. Those ingredients, in the end, come together as hard work.

There's just no way around it if you want to change your current life or work situation. Consider the following comments:

"Hard work is the primary ingredient of success. There are no shortcuts."[6]

Blogger John Bossong

"Having recently concluded four years of interviews for a book on the topic of making ideas happen, I can say one thing for sure: Hard work is the single greatest competitive advantage. Ideas don't happen because they are great. The genius is in the execution, aka the "99% perspiration" . . . "[7]

Scott Belsky
VP of Community, Adobe

So, what's your answer? Are you willing to work hard? Don't answer too quickly! "Yes" is easy to say. It's the follow-through that's difficult. If you'll discipline yourself to work hard along with being a continual learner (key question #1), you'll be half way to changing and improving your professional situation.

Don't stop half way! Keep pushing forward to the next questions. And the next chapter.

9

Question #3

We established earlier in the book that perhaps you didn't plan on being where you are today. Life may have taken some turns, maybe knocked you back a time or two, and now you find yourself asking: "Is this all there is?"

Well, you're not alone. Many people have walked a similar path before you, and yet, some of them ended up being some of the most famous, successful people in the world!

Henry Ford—This pioneer of modern business and production at one point found himself fired from his first car company. Can you imagine how he was feeling when his investors lost confidence in him and shuttered the company after just a year and a half? Just a year later Ford tried again and met the same fate. But Ford pushed forward yet again and this time started Ford Motor Company which we have today.

Walt Disney—Certainly Walt Disney didn't suffer any setbacks, did he? Well, before starting the Disney empire, Walt was actually fired from the Kansas City Star Newspaper at a young age. Why? He wasn't creative enough. In 1922, Walt started his own company to develop cartoons and short advertising films. A year after starting, Laugh-O-Gram went bankrupt. Walt then moved to Hollywood to start The Walt Disney Company.

Oprah Winfrey—Before Oprah became one of the most successful and famous media and entertainment professionals ever, Oprah suffered several setbacks, including being fired several times. In fact, she was once fired as a TV reporter because she was "unfit for television."

Bill Gates, co-founder of Microsoft and one of the richest people in the world, failed at his first company. Steve Jobs founded Apple, was fired, and returned years later to make it the most valuable company in the world.

While these stories may be extreme, they are great examples of our third question for success and a chance to change your current career trajectory. And just like the first two questions, the answer to Question #3 is yes. Ready? Ask yourself this:

Am I willing to work hard?

"Wait a minute, this must be a mistake. Didn't I just read this? Isn't this question #2?" Well, yes, you did read this in the previous chapter. But it's question #3 as well.

Hard work is so critical to career (and life) success that it deserves repeating. And I'm not the only one pounding the "work hard" drum:[1]

"I'm a real hard worker. I work and work and work all the time."

Martha Stewart

"It's all hard work. Nothing comes easily."

Rupert Murdoch
Media tycoon

"We work our fingers to the bone."

Dave Lavery
NASA engineer

"I wasn't the funniest guy growing up, but I was the guy who worked on being funny the hardest."

Chris Rock
Comedian

Here again, maybe extreme examples using extremely successful people but the end result is the same—working hard is the key to success.

"Yeah, whatever. I'm not as talented as Chris Rock or as smart as a NASA engineer." Are you thinking that? If so, STOP! Don't get me wrong. Are Chris Rock, Martha Stewart, and Oprah Winfrey talented? Yes. Are Dave Lowery and Bill Gates smart? Absolutely! But that doesn't mean you must be super-smart and extremely talented to be successful. Educator Richard St. John says, "We overestimate talent and underestimate work. In the end, hard work trumps talent."

Regarding intelligence, St. John commented similarly, "We underestimate work and overestimate smarts. In the end, work wins over smarts." According to St. John, Nez Hallet III agrees with this. Graduating from high school with a C average and college with a C- average, Hallet, CEO of Smart Wireless, says, "If you're going to be successful at anything, the key thing is to work hard."[2]

Are you getting the picture? If you want to change your current situation, you must put some effort into it. Okay, maybe a lot of effort into it! But career success isn't reserved for brain surgeons and Academy-Award winning actors. You can have it as well by simply digging in and working hard.

A slightly different but closely related way to look at hard work is to say grit. When Henry Ford was fired from his first two car companies, he didn't let that stop him. He pushed forward. He worked hard. He showed grit.

So did Walt Disney and Oprah. When they got knocked down, they showed determination and grit, pushed forward, worked hard, and reached unimagined success. You can do the same!

What is grit? According to psychologist Angela Duckworth, who has conducted more research into this area than just about anyone else, "The gritty person approaches achievement as a marathon. The gritty person sticks with it, whereas others might be distracted by boredom, failure, adversity, or plateaus." [3]

Is your adult, professional career a sprint or a marathon? It's a marathon, of course. In fact, it's a 30-, 40-, or sometimes even a 50-year marathon! This long path will require grit, determination, and hard work.

It's Called a Path

Career: A person's progress or general course of action through life, as in some profession or undertaking.

Path: A route, course, or track along which something moves.

Put these two words together and you have your current life situation: progress in your profession along a certain course. Your career path. Pretty easily understood.

A little harder to understand or at least worthy of a short exploration is the idea of career path as a journey or final destination; which is it?

Most people look at career path as a destination, especially when sitting in a specific company seat. For example, if you're reading this book and you're in a frontline call center position, you may be looking at a career path like this:

- Team Lead
- Frontline Manager
- Senior Manager
- AVP
- VP
- SVP
- President!

Is it really possible to reach that last level? **Absolutely!** Here's the key, though—it won't happen overnight. I know you know this but it's worth repeating. A career path like this takes years of hard work. Make no mistake though; this career path is available to anyone!

In this case, career path can be looked at as a destination. This is especially true with older generations. My dad started his first professional job in the mailroom of a major magazine publisher in the energy industry and 30+ years later was the #2 man in the company.

30 years!

Step by step, promotion by promotion, he made his way up through the organization.

Today's average career path doesn't look like that. Whereas 30-year careers with the same company were the norm when my dad was working, those long-term stays don't happen as often today.

What has taken the place of destination as a career path? The journey.

A career journey is similar to the career destination in that you might still start in the mailroom and end up the #2 (or #1!) person in the company like my dad did. Most likely, though, you'll be president of a different mailroom. In other words, you won't have a short resume that lists just one employer for 30 years. You'll have multiple companies and stops along the way to becoming president. Sometimes, your career journey may include multiple stops at the same company and that's okay. If you are a good worker and leave a company well and on good terms, there's no reason you can't return to that company in a position of higher authority.

The important thing is to view your career as a journey, learning something (or many things) at each step along the way. **Enjoy the journey!**

Grit. Determination. Stick-to-itiveness. All terms that are related to our key Question #3: Are you willing to work hard?

It's probably safe to call this a short chapter and bring it to a close. We could keep digging here, exploring the idea of hard work but hopefully you're getting the idea through this chapter along with the previous one. If you want to change your current career situation, move up in your current job, or set out on a different path, there is no substitute for hard work.

So with three of four key questions behind us, let's show grit and work hard as we push forward to the final question.

10

Question #4

Before revealing the fourth and final key question, let's pause:

What are you thinking? Have you started reviewing your career? Have you taken a look at your current situation and found it lacking a bit? Why is that? How did you end up here and what are you willing to do to change your situation? How can communicating better and thinking more help you? Finally, answer this question, "Do I work hard?" The key here is to be honest with yourself. Really, can you call yourself a hard worker? Would others call you a hard worker?

So many questions! And we have one more key question to go. Ready? Hang with me—we're almost done!

As a reminder, here are the first three key questions:

- Am I willing to be a continual learner?

- Am I willing to work hard?

- Am I willing to work hard?

To be successful in work and in life, your answer should be yes to each question. "Yes" should also be your answer to key Question #4:

Am I willing to work hard?

Surprised? Maybe some of you are. Others may have seen this question coming. I hope you don't think I just pulled a "bait and switch." I promised four questions to change your career trajectory. In fact, the book even promised it: *3 + 4 Equals Success*.

But when you come right down to it, you don't need four questions. Success only takes two questions (maybe I should have titled the book *3 + 4 – 2 Equals Success*): will you always learn and will you work hard. It's that simple.

Related to these skills and questions are other ideas and concepts such as showing grit and determination as you explore your career path which we touched on in the revious chapter. Other ideas related to hard work and career success are showing a positive

A Word About Attitude

Dave Kerpen, successful author and keynote speaker, learned an early lesson about hard work and attitude. His first job was selling Crunch 'n Munch during Boston baseball and basketball games. His first night he sold 12 boxes and made a whopping $15.

Not satisfied, he came to work the second night not as a ballpark vendor but as an entertainer. A little singing, a little dancing, a lot of screaming and goofiness. The result? He sold 36 boxes. After stepping up his efforts even more, he became known as the "Crunch 'n Munch Guy." He actually started autographing each box of Crunch 'n Munch and was featured in local newspapers and TV stations. Kerpen even made his way on to ESPN Sportscenter! At his peak, Kerpen was signing up to 300 boxes a night and clearing between $400 and $500 nightly![1]

So his attitude played a huge difference in his work. He wasn't just a ballpark vendor—he was an entertainer!

Attitude plus lots of hard work is a combination that works for anyone! How can a positive attitude improve your work life?

attitude and having a strong character. All are critical things that have an impact on your life and career.

You can have a positive outlook on life and have good character but still not be where you want to be in your life. You still have to go out every day, do the hard things, and push past the challenges. This might mean answering the phone 100 or even 200 times a day. It could mean putting up with customers that yell at you and call you names. It could mean working under a boss that doesn't like you or value you.

Hard work happens at all stages in life. In fact, counter to what many young people are experiencing today, many times hard work starts at an early age. Ashton Kutcher had this to say at the 2013 Teen Choice Awards:

> "I believe that opportunity looks a lot like hard work. When I was 13, I had my first job with my dad, carrying shingles up to the roof, and then I got a job washing dishes at a restaurant, and then I got a job in a grocery store deli, and then I got a job at a factory sweeping Cheerio dust off the ground."

> "And I've never had a job in my life that I was better than. I was always just lucky to have a job. And every job I had was a stepping stone to my next job, and I never quit my job until I had my next job. And so opportunities look a lot like work."[2]

Wow! Strong words from someone who makes success look easy.

Building "Hard Work Muscles"

If you've ever gone to the gym over an extended period of time, you learn that the hard things become easier. When you first start working out—lifting weights, running on a treadmill, sweating through a jazzercise class—it's hard. In fact, you may not make it all the way through that jazzercise class! After taking a day off to let your muscles recover, you return to the gym. It's probably still hard and you still don't make it through that jazzercise class or do those 12 bench presses, but after hitting the gym three, four, maybe five times, you notice something. It's not as painful as when you started. You can do an extra bench press or two. You almost make it through the entire jazzercise class.

After nine or ten classes? You're getting through the entire jazzercise routine and you're ready to increase the weight on the bench press. You notice that with time, exercising gets easier, and you feel better!

The same is true for your "hard work muscles." Go to work tomorrow with a different attitude. Give it 100% effort all day. Extend friendship and grace to that coworker that drives you crazy. Offer to help your boss with something – ANYTHING – that might make his/her day easier. By the end of the day, you may get tired and even revert to a "I-really-don't-want-to-be-here" attitude. Go home, get some rest, eat a good dinner, and exhibit that hard work attitude tomorrow. Over time, just like the gym, your days will get easier.

You'll start getting more work done and getting more out of work. Your hard work will result in people, bosses and coworkers alike, noticing your efforts. You even start looking forward to hard work and new challenges because you know the result will be career growth. You begin controlling your life rather than letting life push you around.

You are in the driver's seat!

If you want to change your life situation, if you want to be happier and more satisfied with your career, you must work hard. To take your career to levels unseen, you must not simply work hard but love to work hard. Hard work is what separates the haves and have-nots. It also separates the good from the great.

The sooner you start running toward hard work instead of away from it, the sooner you'll begin moving toward your career goals and the benefits that come with it. Dr. Joel Gardner, professor of Instructional Design at Franklin University, noticed these benefits and career progress as a result of hard work. "[My career] has been a difficult process filled with a great deal of hard work and sacrifice, but I am now enjoying many of the blessings that come from that hard work, and I am excited to keep moving forward in my career."[3]

The Larry Bird Work Ethic

Larry Bird: One of the greatest basketball players to ever hit the court. Certainly he had some skill and physical abilities that allowed him to play the game. But Bird did more than play the game—he was one of the best!

What made him great? Hard work.

When Larry Bird played basketball, players were required to arrive at the basketball arena 90 minutes before game time. By the time most players even entered the arena, Bird was already on the court and had been for some time.

All alone in Boston Garden except for some arena attendants and maybe a few fans, Bird would start shooting free throws. After about ten, he moved out a few feet and start tossing up more shots at a consistent, comfortable pace, as a coach would pass him the basketballs. Bird would then speed up his routine, throwing up shots in rapid-fire sequence. Bird commented once, "I really don't count my shots. I just shoot until I feel good." Normally, that pre-game practice session would include over 300 shots![4]

Yes, Larry Bird had talent to play basketball, but it was his hard work, day in and day out, that made him great. As mentioned earlier, hard work trumps talent.

What does hard work look like for you? Let's start with an example of what it doesn't look like. Let's say your call center shift starts at 8:00 a.m. If you run across the parking lot, flash your badge at security, sprint to your desk, throw your headset over your ears, and through your panting breaths say, "Good morning. How may I help you?", you're not working hard. You may do a hard sprint from the parking lot to your chair, but that's not hard work.

Of course there are times when we arrive just in time to take that first call but those times should be a rare exception. Hard work looks more like arriving at 7:45, saying hi to coworkers, getting that first cup of coffee, checking in with the boss, putting the headset on, and with a smile greeting that first customer.

That hard work continues by sticking to your daily work schedule, being aware of your performance and doing everything possible to meet your goals, assisting your coworkers with tough situations, helping new hires settle into the group, and going out of your way to make your manager look good to their boss. Some would argue this work description is the minimum expectation, that it's not actually hard work, it's simply being professional.

Sadly, and worrisome for business, is the decline in professionalism. According to The Center for Professional Excellence at York College of Pennsylvania, a lack of professional attitude and behavior is a growing concern among HR and business professionals. Asked about the worst professional problems noticed among new employees, survey respondents cited the following four concerns: "lack of urgency in getting a job done, a sense of entitlement, poor performance coupled with a mediocre work ethic, and poor attendance." Other abuses included poor time management, social media abuses such as tweeting or posting on social networks during work, and excessive personal phone calls.[5]

Showing up on time and doing your job well makes you a professional. Showing up a bit early, doing *everything* you can to make yourself and those around you successful, and doing this daily, now you're working hard.

So you see, if you want to make a difference in your career, be happy, satisfied, and reach new levels of success, there are really only two questions you need to ask yourself:

"Am I willing to invest in my career by learning new things?"

"Am I willing to work hard to get to my definition of success?"

Two short questions. Easy to ask. Easy to answer. But hard to follow through on both.

So, how do you do it? How does someone learn constantly and work harder, especially if they think they are already working as hard as they can? That's a great question and I'm glad you asked! If you're ready, take a breath, turn the page, and let's explore the answer to this question in our final chapter.

11

Putting it all together

WOOHOO! You've made it to the end. Well, almost the end. Over these last few pages, we're going to:

- Review what we've learned so far.

- Explore how to put this book into practice.

- Examine a potential roadblock.

A Personal Story

3 + 4 Equals Success.

Three skills.

Four questions (well, two, but you get the idea).

Regularly practice these three skills and consistently ask yourself these four questions and you can change your life. How do I know? Because I've seen it and I've read about successful people who have done it for years.

As mentioned earlier in the book, there is really nothing new here. These ideas of thinking, communicating, valuing, learning, and working hard have been written about for years. There's really nothing new under the "how do I become successful" sun. So why add yet another book to the already-long list of career and self-improvement books? Because we need to read about these concepts again and again and again. In these pages, I hope I have added a bit of a different perspective on these ideas, in a way that will make them interesting for some people to read and spur them to action. These are timeless truths that work, but many of us (all of us?) stray away from these ideas at some point in our life.

We established early in the book that if you're working in a call center, in a back office somewhere, maybe in a restaurant or as a janitor or housekeeper, chances are you weren't planning on being there. Yet there you are..........

Perhaps it's time to reinvent yourself. That's what I've done several times over the course of my career by practicing the skills and having the mindsets that we've discussed in this book.

I spent a large part of my business years in sales and marketing in the information technology industry. For years, I enjoyed helping computer companies of all sizes market their products and services. Of course, what helped me to be successful here was my ability to communicate, which has always been a strength I've enjoyed.

Even though it was a strength, there were many, many people who were much, much better than me. So I practiced. And practiced. And practiced. When I had a chance to participate in a public speaking course, I did. In fact, I took all kinds of training across a number of different skills. I have always tried to be a continuous learner.

I tried to expand my knowledge and skills by reading a lot, talking to many people, and watching the news and other educational TV. I was always open to new ideas and concepts.

I have also tried to engage my brain, to be a good thinker. Of course I have made mistakes, but I've tried to minimize these mistakes by using common sense and making good decisions.

I understood that my success was dependent on those around me so I would go out of my way to help others and was always appreciative of the help they gave me.

I worked hard. Were there times when I backed off or was even lazy. Sure. But when I caught my work ethic slipping, I would turn away from that bad attitude and push ahead in my work and career journey.

Then one day I found myself actually working for one of those computer companies. Actually, it was a software reseller and I managed a large group of business development people. I had reinvented myself.

3 + 4 Equals Success.

> If you work hard enough and assert yourself, and use your mind and imagination, you can shape the world to your desires.
> **Malcolm Gladwell**
> *Outliers: The Story of Success*

For the next few years I continued thinking more, communicating more and valuing people. I tried learning more and working harder. And then came my next reinvention. This time it was a pretty radical change. My beautiful bride and I, along with our three boys, moved to Bulgaria where I was a teacher and then the headmaster of a small, English-speaking school. While I wasn't an educator by trade, I was able to pick up the skills necessary to run a small school and was blessed to have some very competent teachers to carry the teaching load. After an incredible four years, we returned to the United States for yet another reinvention.

This time my entrepreneurial itch needed scratching so I formed a nonprofit organization, NexGen Leadership, to teach life skills, leadership, and faith to high school and college students. While it is still a functioning organization (you can visit it at www.nexgenleadership.org), it was definitely a nonprofit—as in we weren't making any money! And since the family enjoyed having dinner on the table every night, it was time to get a "real" job.

Fortunately, for my entire adult life, I had been practicing 3 + 4, which allowed me to enjoy success in a new field, corporate learning and development. I was now able to put into practice many of the skills I had learned and practiced throughout most of my adult life. First as a Director of Training and later as a Vice President of Culture and Engagement.

My current career stop is with ProCulture Consulting, a speaking and training organization I started recently. Combining everything we've explored in this book—communication, people, thinking, learning, hard work—I hope to find great success with this new venture.

I'm In, But How?

Are you with me? Does all of this make sense? I've thrown a lot at you in just a few pages. In addition to three skills and four questions, we've explored a number of other concepts including the steps to making good decisions, steps to becoming an effective communicator and a good listener, how to appreciate people more and how to become a continual learner.

That's a lot! Do I really expect you to do all of these things?

Well, yes, I do.

Of course, you can't do everything right now. But you can start working on a few items and as you become proficient at them, start working on a few more. We mentioned the ability to prioritize earlier in the book. Practice that skill now by reviewing the book, picking a few areas where you could use improvement, and starting that improvement process. The most important thing at this point is to START!

As you begin your march to becoming a better employee and a better person, let me leave you with two thoughts (this is the last list—I promise!).

You Must Choose

Choice. It's a word we've hit several times throughout this book. You already made one choice by choosing to read this book. If you've made it this far, then there's something inside you telling you these ideas and concepts are important. There's something inside you that's saying, "It's time for a change." That's awesome! Keep listening to that little voice.

If you are dissatisfied with your life or any particular area of your life, doesn't that beg for a change? When you make different choices, you will be choosing a different life. Think about it. Choosing to approach life differently, taking control of your career, doing "life" and career differently, things can't help but change!

No one else can do this but you. No one can make you think more or communicate better. No one can make you a learner and no one can make you choose a strong work ethic. Only you can make these decisions.

Be prepared for some of your decisions to pay immediate dividends. For example, adjust your sleep schedule so you can get a full night's sleep while also getting up a little earlier than you have been. Your quick payback will be better health and more energy. Your boss and coworkers will notice your extra morning energy as well as the earlier arrival at your desk.

Some choices, though, won't pay back for years. Boxer Sugar Ray Leonard realized this when he was growing up and going to school. After getting his siblings on the school bus, Leonard would run behind the bus all the way to school. People thought he was crazy—really crazy! But Sugar Ray had a dream and knew that it would take years of hard work before he could realize that dream. He was willing to make those hard choices today in order to reach that dream. "I did it because I didn't just want to be better than the next guy, I wanted to be better than all the guys."[1]

Discipline is the Key

We've already established that there is a lot to think about in this book. And maybe you've chosen to work on several of these areas and answer yes to our two key success questions. Do the days ahead seem a bit daunting? Probably. So what will help you move forward? Self-discipline.

Author, blogger, and executive coach Tommy Newberry says this about self-discipline:[2]

"Self-discipline is the ability to funnel your desires and passions in a productive direction, for a sustained period of time in order to achieve your goals."

"Self-discipline helps you synchronize your goals with your choices and keep you moving in the direction of your desired objective. It is developed by moving forward one step at a time and creating momentum in small, daily acts."

That last sentence is key. "Moving forward one step at a time and creating momentum in small, daily acts." You don't have to change overnight and become this super-charged employee who thinks, talks, and values better than everyone else. Your progress is measured over the long haul with small, daily steps.

Newberry also said, "Self-discipline is the connective tissue that links ambition with achievement."[3] If you've said yes to the ideas and concepts in this book, then it's self-discipline that will connect your desire with reality. In other words, self-discipline will connect your heart (desire) with your head (reality).

Research published in the Journal of Personality concluded that self-disciplined people are happier and enjoy more long-term contentment that people with less self-discipline.

A Potential Roadblock.

Hopefully, you've enjoyed this book and have caught wind of the positive vibe. While I hate to interrupt that positive sentiment, I feel it's important to acknowledge a troubling point.

We have identified three skills to practice and offered four (okay, two) simple questions to which the correct answer is yes. We have also identified the fact that committing to those skills and saying yes to those questions is the easy part. Through self-discipline, you can bring about positive change to your work situation.

Here's the sad news—not everyone reading this book will answer yes to our two key questions. Some people will choose to ignore those skills, either saying they already do them well (that may be so but everyone has room for improvement) or simply dismiss them as unnecessary. For those of you in this category, let me put the challenge out there once more.

Don't settle. That's my challenge. If you are less than happy with your current professional situation, logic says you need to make a change. Unless you want to stay unhappy, why wouldn't you make a change? Doesn't doing something differently in order to find happiness and job satisfaction seem like the right path?

Others reading this book will look at the skills needed or the amount of work necessary to change things and simply give up. The work and the effort are just too hard.

You might be right—the work may be hard. But big things almost always require big effort. Sometimes you may get lucky and find instant success. This luck is rare, however, and does not produce the long-lasting satisfaction that effort creates.

So, keep your eyes on the prize even if it's years away. You will feel good about yourself regardless of reaching your goal. Simply making your best effort produces its own reward. Hitting your goals just adds to that satisfaction!

I hope I'm wrong. I hope everyone reading this book starts practicing self-discipline by simply getting to this point in the book! If you are reading these words, then there's something that's ringing true in your mind and your heart. Don't let this moment pass. Seize the energy and momentum you have created by picking up this book and push forward to becoming a new you.

You will not be disappointed.

12

Parting thoughts

When I started the previous chapter with "WOOHOO! You've made it to the end," I really thought it was the final chapter. However, two things have prompted me to write one more chapter, a flight from Ontario, California, back to my home in Dallas and an unsettled feeling at the end of the last chapter. Allow me to first address that unsettled feeling.

I hope you have sensed a positive, upbeat tone throughout this book. That was certainly my intent. So after I wrote that cautionary note about readers choosing not to pursue this life of career advancement and satisfaction, well, I just couldn't end on that downer note.

I hope I'm wrong. I hope everyone reads this book and is inspired to go to new heights not only in their career but also in their personal life. As was mentioned earlier in the book, the concepts presented here are not difficult so understanding the information isn't the problem. Implementing these ideas and skills is where the difficulty arises.

That's the bad news. The good news, though, is that ANYONE and EVERYONE can summon the discipline to make this happen. I've seen it time and time again.

Don't let the amount of information presented in the book overwhelm you. Yes, we covered a lot of ground in these pages. Thinking, communicating, and valuing—three skills critical to your career success. We spent time on two questions, will you always learn and will you work hard. Sprinkled among these skills and questions are multiple lists and "To Dos" for career and life success. There is a list of people skills, a strategy for making good decisions, and ideas for brainstorming sessions.

Putting these concepts, skills, and ideas to work will put you on the road to success. There is, however, one obstacle that stands in your way. One tiny thing that stands between where you are today and where you want to be one, five, or ten years from now.

Choice.

We briefly touched on this concept earlier in the book but it's worth repeating.

A small, five-letter word yet it contains so much power. You use that power dozens if not hundreds of times per day. You choose your attitude—positive or negative—each morning shortly after waking up. You choose to be (or not to be) on time at work. You choose to have a happy, positive attitude at work—or not. On your way home, you choose to let the other driver merge into traffic in front of you or you choose to speed up a bit, cut him off, and let him merge in behind you.

Those are all your choices.

Putting into practice the information presented in these pages is also a choice. No one can force you or make this decision for you. It's completely up to you whether or not you want to start pushing the career accelerator or stay stuck in neutral (at best).

Want to change your life circumstances? Make different choices. In fact, that makes a pretty good life motto, doesn't it?

Change Your Choices—Change Your Life.

I hope you choose to put your career into overdrive by adding these ideas and concepts. You'll be glad you did!

The Important Questions

In Chapter 1, you were presented with the following questions:

- "Am I happy here?"
- "Why am I still here?"
- "Is this all there is for the rest of my life?"
- "Where do I go from here?"
- "Does it matter that I am here?"
- "Can I make a difference while I am here?"

I hope the chapters that followed have helped you answer those questions. While they are all important, I'm wondering if the first and last might hold a little extra significance.

That thought just occurred to me as I write these final words on my way back to Dallas after celebrating my mother-in-law's 80th birthday. It is painfully obvious that the flight attendant who just handed me a Diet Coke is not happy. Maybe she's had a bad day. Maybe she's heading home after a long trip. Maybe her mind is focusing on a pressing personal issue.

Perhaps, on the other hand, she's just not happy with her job. She doesn't smile, is not very pleasant, and seems to simply go through the motions of her tasks, handing out water and drinks with all of the emotion of a dead fish.

Why does she keep on working as a flight attendant? Sure, the benefits of flying free are great. But are those occasional free flights across the country worth all of the long hours spent doing a job that she doesn't believe in or doesn't like?

That's the first question. Now, what about the last? Could this flight attendant make a difference on that flight? Absolutely! First, her poor attitude will have an impact on my choice of future air travel. While I may not change airlines based on one grumpy flight attendant, I will file this experience in the back of my mind and should I run across grumpy flight attendants or other airline personnel on future flights, at some point I'll take my business elsewhere.

Second and more importantly, this flight attendant certainly could have made my flight home a little more cheery. It was a great trip and nothing will change that fact, but when my wife casually mentioned the poor attitude that she also noticed, well, we both had a "that was a bummer" comment about our trip home.

So please answer all of those questions but when you think about your happiness and the difference you can make to those around you, well, you might want to spend a few extra minutes on those two questions.

Congratulations!

You made it. Just a few short paragraphs and you're done. My hope is the words and pages in this book make a difference in your life.

There are many life skills you need to practice if you want to be successful. Goal setting, time management, and self-responsibility to name a few. But without the skills presented in this book, your task of reaching higher and higher levels of professional success will be difficult at best if not outright impossible.

What about hard work? There is no substitute. There are no shortcuts. It is the primary ingredient to success. You can be the best at the life skills presented in this book and you will certainly enjoy some benefits and see some career success. However, without the hard work to back up these skills, you will fall well short of any ideas of success you have in your mind.

Let me leave you with a final thought. You may think it's too late to reinvent yourself. You are too old or too set in your ways. If this is you, I have one word.

STOP!

Stop that kind of self-defeating thinking. You can do this. It's never too late to try something new, to search for that happiness and satisfaction that comes with doing a job well and

> The best time to plant a tree is twenty years ago. The second best time is now.
> **Chinese Proverb**

enjoying the work that you do.

> **A year from now you may wish you had started today.**
>
> **Karen Lamb**
> **Author**

The best time to set a course for job happiness and satisfaction is today!

As you meet your career goals and find new professional success and satisfaction, I would love to hear from you. So visit our website: www.procultureconsulting.com, and tell us your success story. We can't wait to hear from you.

Now, go take on the day!

Answers to thinking questions

Before Mt. Everest was discovered, what was the highest mountain in the world?

Mt. Everest

Johnny's mother had three children. The first child was named April. The second child was named May. What was the third child's name?

Johnny

In British Columbia, you cannot take a picture of a man with a wooden leg. Why not?

Wooden legs can't take pictures You need a camera (or a smartphone!)

A clerk at a butcher shop stands five feet ten inches tall and wears a size 13 sneakers. What does he weigh?

He weighs meat. After all, he's a butcher!

About the Author

After earning a Bachelor's degree in Marketing from the University of Tulsa, Darren embarked on a career that has crossed several industries as well as continents.

Darren's early career was in the IT industry selling advertising and marketing services to some of the IT industry's biggest players including Dell Computer and Compaq Computer (now known as Hewlett-Packard).

Darren left the IT industry to partner with two friends, starting a training company based on Southwest Airlines principles. After a successful launch, Darren and his family felt called to give a little back to society so they moved to Sofia, Bulgaria, where Darren became headmaster of a small English-speaking school.

Four years later, Darren and his family returned to the U.S. and founded NexGen Leadership, a nonprofit organization dedicated to teaching leadership and life skills to high school and college students. While still leading NexGen, Darren later joined a leading auto finance company, first as Director of Employee Development and then transitioning to VP Culture & Engagement. After spending two years with this organization, Darren was driven to launch yet another new business, ProCulture Consulting that he still leads today.

Darren is uniquely qualified to write and teach about career progression. Darren has enjoyed career success throughout his professional life. Using the concepts and skills presented throughout this book, Darren has reinvented himself several times, taking on career challenges in new fields and even new countries.

Darren also has experience working across generations and is President of NexGen Leadership, a nonprofit dedicated to presenting these career philosophies to high school and college students and helping them find career success. You can learn more about NGL by visiting their website at www.nexgenleadership.org.

Whether working with frontline call center employees, mid-level managers, executives, or Millennials just entering the workforce, Darren's entertaining and personable style allows him to connect and engage with his audience. His inspiring messages will motivate employees to work hard and perform at their greatest ability.

For more information about Darren and ProCulture Consulting, visit www.procultureconsulting.com.

ProCulture Consulting

Want to challenge your employees to become People Improvement Professionals? Bring Darren and ProCulture Consulting directly to your organization.

Spending an hour listening to Darren explore the three essential work skills and four crucial questions outlined in *3 + 4 = Success* will motivate workers to view their work, their co-workers, and their customers differently. Spending an interactive afternoon diving deeply into these topics will help your organization take those next steps in building an engaged workforce and healthy corporate culture.

In addition to exploring how employees can grow their career and find job satisfaction and meaning, ProCulture Consulting offers additional business programs.

- Keynote Presentation Topics (60-90 minutes)
- Managing The Millennial Generation
- I'm a Millennial—How Do I Fit In Here?
- Delivering "Wow" Customer Service
- How To Avoid The Coming Leadership Crisis
- Becoming an Employer of Choice—The Benefits of a Healthy Corporate Culture

Half-day or Full day workshops (2-, 4-, or 8-hour programs)

Go deeper into any of the ProCulture Consulting keynote presentations by spending extended time exploring ideas and strategies. Each interactive workshop includes participant workbooks and offers attendees the opportunity to discuss these critical business topics in great detail, resulting in changed behavior and higher performance. In addition to the above topics, PCC also offers:

- Effective Presentation Skills
- Take Your Call Center From Good To Great

For more information, visit:

PCC at **www.procultureconsulting.com**

Notes

Chapter 1: I'm gonna be an astronaut!

1. Wikipedia, Apollo 11, http://en.wikipedia.org/wiki/*Apollo 11*.

2. http://en.wikipedia.org/wiki/Apollo_11.

3. Levo League, *Why You Should Take Your Childhood Dream Job Seriously*, http://www.levoleague.com/articles/uncategorized/childhood-dream-job (January 25, 2013).

4. http://www.levoleague.com/articles/uncategorized/childhood-dream-job.

5. Top 15 Kids' Dream Jobs, About.com, http://jobsearch.about.com/od/kids/ss/top-15-kids-dream-jobs.htm.

6. Deanna Dewberry, *Call Center Jobs Returning To The U.S., Bringing Jobs to DFW*, http://www.nbcdfw.com/investigations/Call-Center-Jobs-Returning-to-US-Bringing-Jobs-to-DFW-196516711.html (March 9, 2013).

7. Jon Acuff, Start. (Brentwood, Tennessee: Lampo Press, 2013), 10.

8. Acuff, 15.

9. http://www.goodreads.com/quotes/48122-the-brick-walls-are-there-for-a-reason-the-brick

Chapter 2: I am NOT a Contact Center Representative.

1. http://www.brainyquote.com/quotes/authors/o/og_mandino.html.

2. http://www.brainyquote.com/quotes/authors/o/oprah_winfrey_2.html.

3. Teresa Amabile, Steve Kramer, *What Makes Work Worth Doing*, HBR Blog Network, http://blogs.hbr.org/2012/08/what-makes-work-worth-doing/

4. (August 31, 2012).

5. http://www.brainyquote.com/quotes/topics/topic_work.html#6P5Kp8418ElkgcTT.99.

6. Richard Citron, *Are You In or Out?*, Courageous Leadership, http://www.citrinconsulting.com/wp-content/newsletter/feb-2011.php (February 2011).

7. Team Building and Teamwork Quotes, teampedia, http://www.teampedia.net/wiki/index.php?title=Team_Building_and_Teamwork_Quotes.

Chapter 4 - Three Keys To Success

1. Acuff, 51.

2. IBM Corporation, "Capitalizing on Complexity; Insights from the Global Chief Executive Officer Study", 2010, p. 3.

3. Institute for the Future for the University of Phoenix Research Institute, "Future Work Skills 2020", 2011, pp. 9-10.

4. Don Metznik, 25 *Famous Quotations About Strategy*, Business Strategy and Marketing Solutions, http://www.metznik.com/blog/bid/56358/25-Famous-Quotations-About-Strategy (November 14, 2012).

5. Mike Myatt, "A Crisis Of Leadership – What's Next?", Forbes, October 10, 2013, http://www.forbes.com/sites/mikemyatt/2013/10/10/a-crisis-of-leadership-whats-next/#!.

Chapter 5 – What Are You Talking About?

1. Jeff Thompson, *Is Nonverbal Communications a Numbers Game?*, Psychology Today, http://www.psychologytoday. com/blog/beyond-words/201109/is-nonverbal-communi- cation-numbers-game (September 30, 2011).

2. John Coleman, "For Those Who Want to Lead, Read", Harvard Business Review, August 15, 2012.

3. Anne Kreamer, "The Business Case for Reading Novels", Harvard Business Review, January 11, 2012.

4. Kyle Wiens, "I Won't Hire People Who Use Poor Gram- mar. Here's Why.", Harvard Business Review, July 20, 2012.

5. Nick Bilton, *Disruptions: More Connected, Yet More Alone, Bits*, http://bits.blogs.nytimes.com/2013/09/01/disrup- tions-more-connected-yet-more-alone/?_r=2 (September 1, 2013).

6. April Dembosky, "Cerebral Circuitry", Financial Times, January 3, 2013.

7. Pau Hammerness, Margaret Moore, "Train Your Brain to Focus", Harvard Business Review, January 18.2012.

Chapter 6 – What do you value?

1. http://www.brainyquote.com/quotes/quotes/r/ralph- marst163841.html.

2. Jay Hart, *Phil Mickelson makes little boy's day*, Yahoo Sports, http://sports.yahoo.com/blogs/golf-devil-ball-golf/phil- mickelson-makes-little-boy-day-144119857.html;_ylt=Aw- rTWfy_8ttS_mUABhVNbK5, July 18, 2013.

3. Institute for the Future for the University of Phoenix Re- search Institute, "Future Work Skills 2020", 2011, p. 8.

4. Peter F. Drucker, "Managing Onself"," *Best of Harvard Business Review* (January 2005): 100-109.

Chapter 7: It's Time To Answer Some Questions

1. http://www.brainyquote.com/quotes/authors/o/oliver_wendell_holmes_2.html

2. Rick Rigsby, *Living On Purpose*, Rick Rigsby, http://www.rickrigsby.com/index.cfm/rick-rigsby-blog/living-on-purpose/, March-April 2013.

3. Institute for the Future for the University of Phoenix Research Institute, "Future Work Skills 2020", 2011, pp. 11-12.

4. Bill Taylor, *Are You Learning as Fast as the World Is Changing?*, HBR Blog Network, http://blogs.hbr.org/2012/01/are-you-learning-as-fast-as-th/, January 26, 2012.

5. Ron Shaich, *If You're Learning, You'll Never Need to Recharge*, Linkedin, http://www.linkedin.com/today/post/article/20130606150602-25745675-if-you-re-learning-you-ll-never-need-to-recharge?ref=email, June 6, 2013

6. Coleman.

Chapter 8 – Question #2

1. Douglas Merrill, *Why Multitasking Doesn't Work*, Forbes, http://www.forbes.com/sites/douglasmerrill/2012/08/17/why-multitasking-doesnt-work/, August 17, 2012.

1. *Top 25 Work Ethic Quotes*, MoveMe "Quotes", http://www.movemequotes.com/top-25-work-ethic-quotes/.

1. Liz Klimas, *Restaurant Owner Finds Dedicated Teen Walking 10 Snowy Miles For Job Interview – Guess Where He's Working Now*, The Blaze, http://www.theblaze.com/stories/2013/02/25/restaurant-owner-finds-dedicated-teen-walking-10-snowy-miles-for-job-interview-guess-where-hes-working-now/, February 25, 2013

1. Tony Dungy, *Uncommon: Finding Your Path to Significance*, (Winter Park, Florida: Tyndale, 2009), pp. 6-7.

1. Jon Gordon, as quoted in Jamie Eckle, *Career Watch: The benefits of hard work*, Computerworld, http://www.computerworld.com/s/article/344194/Career_Watch. October 19, 2009.

1. John Bossong, *2 Key Benefits of Hard Work, Leadership, Sales, & Life:* A Blog by John Bossong, http://johnbossong.com/2013/05/17/3-key-benefits-of-hard-work/, May 17, 2013.

1. Scott Belsky, *Hard Work: What's It Good For?*, 99U: Insights on making ideas happen, http://99u.com/articles/6623/hard-work-whats-it-good-for, date unavailable

Chapter 9 – Question #3

1. Richard St. John, *Why it pays to work hard*, TedEd: Lessons Worth Sharing, http://ed.ted.com/lessons/richard-st-john-why-it-pays-to-work-hard#review, date unavailable.

2. Richard St. John.

3. Angela Duckworth, Angela Duckworth talks to IC, incharacter: A Journal of Everyday Virtues, http://incharacter.org/features/angela-duckworth-talks-to-ic/, April 1, 2009.

4. Aimee Groth, Student Test Scores Show That 'Grit' Is More Important Than IQ, Business Insider, http://www.businessinsider.com/grit-is-more-important-than-iq-2013-5, May 28, 2013.

Chapter 10 – Question #4

1. Dave Kerpen, Your Attitude at Work is Everything, LinkedIn, http://www.linkedin.com/today/post/article/20130304154223-15077789-how-to-give-yourself-a-promotion-at-work, March 4, 2013.

2. John Howerton, *Famous Actor Reveals Real Name, Gives Incredibly Insightful Speech About 'Hard Work' And Generosity.*

. . *At Teen Choice Awards,* The Blaze, http://www.theblaze.com/stories/2013/08/13/famous-actor-reveals-real-name-gives-incredibly-insightful-speech-about-hard-work-and-generosity-at-teen-choice-awards/, August 13, 2013.

3. Joel Gardner, *To Reach Career Goals, Be Deliberate, Reflections on Learning Success*, http://joelleegardner.blogspot.com/2013/07/to-reach-career-goals-be-deliberate.html, July 8, 2013.

4. Bob Starkey, *The Larry Bird Work Ethic*, Hoop Thoughts, http://hoopthoughts.blogspot.com/2009/05/larry-bird-work-ethic.html, May 12, 2009.

5. Lin Grensing-Pophal, How's Your Professionalism?, SHRM HR Careers, http://www.shrm.org/HRCareers/Pages/0212professionalism.aspx, date unavailable.

Chapter 11 – Putting It All Together

1. Alex Banayan, Five Traits of Wildly Successful People, LinkedIn, http://www.linkedin.com/today/post/article/20131011051941-80844253-the-5-traits-of-wildly-successful-people?trk=tod-home-art-list-large_0, October 11, 2013.

2. Tommy Newberry, *Discipline Yourself: Becoming a World-Class Success*, Tommy Newberry, http://www.tommynewberry.com/discipline-yourself-becoming-a-world-class-success/, August 16, 2012.

3. Tommy Newberry.